Organize

IN SEARCH OF MEDIA

Götz Bachmann, Timon Beyes, Mercedes Bunz,
and Wendy Hui Kyong Chun, Series Editors

Pattern Discrimination

Markets

Communication

Machine

Remain

Archives

Organize

Organize

**Timon Beyes, Lisa Conrad,
and Reinhold Martin**

Afterword by Geert Lovink and Ned Rossiter

IN SEARCH OF MEDIA

University of Minnesota Press
Minneapolis
London

meson press

In Search of Media is a collaboration between the
University of Minnesota Press and meson press,
an open access publisher, https://meson.press/.

Organize by Timon Beyes, Lisa Conrad, and Reinhold
Martin is licensed under a Creative Commons Attribution-
NonCommercial 4.0 International License.

Published by the
University of Minnesota Press, 2019
111 Third Avenue South, Suite 290
Minneapolis, MN 55401-2520
https://www.upress.umn.edu

in collaboration with
meson press
Salzstrasse 1
21335 Lüneburg, Germany
https://meson.press

ISBN 978-1-5179-0805-8 (pb)
A Cataloging-in-Publication record for this book is available
from the Library of Congress.

The University of Minnesota is an equal-opportunity educator
and employer.

UMP BmB

Contents

Series Foreword   vii

Introduction   ix
Timon Beyes, Lisa Conrad, and Reinhold Martin

[1]   Media Organize: Persons   1
Reinhold Martin

[2]   Organizing Media: Security and Entertainment   29
Timon Beyes

[3]   Organization Is the Message: Gray Media   63
Lisa Conrad

Afterword: Propositions on the Organizational Form   89
Geert Lovink and Ned Rossiter

Authors   102

Series Foreword

"Media determine our situation," Friedrich Kittler infamously wrote in his Introduction to *Gramophone, Film, Typewriter.* Although this dictum is certainly extreme—and media archaeology has been critiqued for being overly dramatic and focused on technological developments—it propels us to keep thinking about media as setting the terms for which we live, socialize, communicate, organize, do scholarship, et cetera. After all, as Kittler continued in his opening statement almost thirty years ago, our situation, "in spite or because" of media, "deserves a description." What, then, are the terms—the limits, the conditions, the periods, the relations, the phrases—of media? And, what is the relationship between these terms and determination? This book series, *In Search of Media,* answers these questions by investigating the often elliptical "terms of media" under which users operate. That is, rather than produce a series of explanatory keyword-based texts to describe media practices, the goal is to understand the conditions (the "terms") under which media is produced, as well as the ways in which media impacts and changes these terms.

Clearly, the rise of search engines has fostered the proliferation and predominance of keywords and terms. At the same time, it has changed the very nature of keywords, since now any word and pattern can become "key." Even further, it has transformed the very process of learning, since search presumes that, (a) with the right phrase, any question can be answered and (b) that the answers lie within the database. The truth, in other words, is "in there." The impact of search/media on knowledge, however, goes beyond search engines. Increasingly, disciplines—from sociology to economics, from the arts to literature—are in search of media as a way to revitalize their methods and objects of study. Our current media situation therefore seems to imply a new term, understood as temporal shifts of mediatic conditioning. Most broadly, then, this series asks: What are the terms or conditions of knowledge itself?

To answer this question, each book features interventions by two (or more) authors, whose approach to a term—to begin with: *communication, pattern discrimination, markets, remain, machine, archives*—diverge and converge in surprising ways. By pairing up scholars from North America and Europe, this series also advances media theory by obviating the proverbial "ten year gap" that exists across language barriers due to the vagaries of translation and local academic customs and in order to provoke new descriptions, prescriptions, and hypotheses—to rethink and reimagine what media can and must do.

Introduction

Timon Beyes, Lisa Conrad, and Reinhold Martin

In search of media, one sooner or later arrives at the question of organization. The relation between media and organization is so obvious that it borders on the tautological: after all, media organize things into patterns and relations. As Cornelia Vismann (2008) has shown in her media history *Files*, these seemingly innocuous everyday recording, storing, and circulation apparatuses are at the heart of the legal and administrative systems as we know them. Their techniques have come to shape the architecture of digital machines and data processing, in which we thus find traces of more or less bygone administrative practices. Media can therefore be understood as "civilizational ordering devices" (Peters 2015, 5), and if the civilizational encompasses all kinds of sociotechnical ordering, then "[media] are fundamental constituents of [any form, or any process of] organization" (Peters 2015, 19). It seems hard to find a more clear-cut claim to relevance for thinking media through organization, and organization through media. But this quasi-tautological loop is in need of further scrutiny. It covers up a complex field—perhaps a battlefield—of relations that indeed constitute matters of great concern. In fact, if media are busy ordering social or sociotechnical relations, then they are invested with power and domination, control and surveillance, disruption and emancipation (Lovink and Rossiter 2018).

This intimate relation of media and organization therefore is as old as the hills (Beyes, Holt, and Pias 2019). Yet digital media technologies actualize it and perhaps exacerbate its potentials and conflicts. After all, "digital media traffic less in content, programs, and opinions than in organization, power, and calculation" (Peters 2015, 7). They forcefully remind us that "organization is the message," to quote the title of Lisa Conrad's contribution to this book. They enable and call for new "propositions on the organizational form," as Geert Lovink and Ned Rossiter make clear in their afterword to this volume.

If technological media are amenable to, or support, or condition different organizational forms, however, then this implies that they can let themselves be somewhat formed, or formed in somewhat different ways. The relation between media and organization is quasi-tautological because it is recursive. Indeed, "media organize," as Reinhold Martin (2003) has concretized the claim that media determine our situation (because how could they determine it if not through organizing it?) and as his chapter in this book further elaborates. In some ways, media determine organization. But at the same time, media are organized, and organization in some ways determines media. "Organizing media," to pick up the title of Timon Beyes's contribution to this volume, thus needs to be read in its twofold meaning: media technologies condition life through their organizational effects (at least in the Western world, to return to Vismann [2008, xii, emphasis original], "a life without files, without any recording, a life *off the record,* is simply unthinkable"); at the same time, to take place, to disappear or to be transformed, media technologies are necessarily predicated on organizational constellations (how files have been and are administered— processed, circulated, archived—shaped their trajectories as media). This recursive loop between media and organization is then quasi-tautological because it touches upon the understanding of media themselves: as "not only the conditions of possibility for events" but "in themselves events: assemblages or constellations of certain technologies, fields of knowledge, and social institutions" (Horn 2007, 8).

This book is dedicated to this "knot" of media and organization.
It does not claim to untie this knot, for that would be a grandilo-
quent, impossible project. But it endeavors to disentangle important threads, both conceptually and empirically (as if the two could
be held distinct). In this sense, while each of the following texts can
be read independently from the others, they have been developed
in joint discussion and are meant to hang together and cohere as a
joint response to the question of media as/and organization.

In "Media Organize: Persons," Reinhold Martin shows how such
"media organizing" takes place through the sociotechnical processes of ordering things, knowledge, and people into—discursive,
institutional, social, political, biological—*bodies.* Through the figures
of the person, the machine, and the circle, Martin traces how
media shape, solidify, and perform corporate bodies, personalizing
corporate forms and affects and binding people to its causes. In
"Organizing Media: Security and Entertainment," Timon Beyes dis-
cusses sculptural works by the artist Simon Denny to coax out their
performance of different yet entangled modes of—protocological,
bureaucratic, and entrepreneurial—ordering. These modes shape
a contemporary organizational nexus of persistent consumer and
citizen surveillance in the name of security and consumption, the
"security–entertainment complex." In "Organization Is the Message:
Gray Media," Lisa Conrad takes a closer look at how media research
can engage with the concept of organization by considering the
"gray medium" of enterprise resource planning software. Distinguishing between media as organizing mechanisms, as themselves
entangled with and predicated on institutional and organizational
conditions, and as implicated in the normative question of the
"good organization," Conrad seeks to find a more affirmative
ground on what organization and media can do to each other
than the comparably dark analyses of Martin and Beyes. In their
"Afterword: Propositions on the Organizational Form," Geert Lovink
and Ned Rossiter resolutely call for experimenting with organizational forms (rather than, we might surmise, merely dwelling

on their oppressive effects). Instead of endorsing or analyzing the short-termism and weak ties of social media, the question of organization here resurfaces as an activist one of "sovereign media," directed at newly found commitments that are in need of more stabilized capacities for decision-making and action.

References

Beyes, Timon, Robin Holt, and Claus Pias, eds. 2019. *The Oxford Handbook of Media, Technology, and Organization Studies.* Oxford: Oxford University Press.

Horn, Eva. 2007. "Editor's Introduction: 'There Are No Media.'" *Grey Room* 29: 6–13.

Lovink, Geert, and Ned Rossiter. 2018. *Organization after Social Media.* Colchester, U.K.: Minor Compositions. http://www.minorcompositions.info/?cat=55.

Martin, Reinhold. 2003. *The Organizational Complex: Architecture, Media, and Corporate Space.* Cambridge, Mass.: MIT Press.

Peters, John Durham. 2015. *The Marvelous Clouds: Toward a Philosophy of Elemental Media.* Chicago: University of Chicago Press.

Vismann, Cornelia. 2008. *Files.* Translated by Geoffrey Winthrop-Young. Stanford, Calif.: Stanford University Press.

Media Organize: Persons

Reinhold Martin

Media organize. By this I mean that, as intermediaries among persons and between persons and worlds, media construct patterns and relationships that pose the question of order. They ask us to ask, is there order here? If so, what is its form? What is its source? Thus, insofar as persons operate media, media also help to organize those persons into active, relational bodies. This circularity opens the fields of media archaeology and media studies beyond their now-classical subject matter—gramophone, film, typewriter, their precursors and their descendants—to such an extent that we must risk tautology and say that the term "media" *itself* refers to the set of sociotechnical artifacts and processes that organize things into patterns and relationships. Sociotechnical rather than merely technical, not only to acknowledge the social production of technical things but also, and again risking tautology, to acknowledge the technical production of social relations.

This view modifies—but also ratifies—the decontextualized Kittlerian aphorism that "media determine our situation" (Kittler 1986). For it is not a question of linear, mechanistic determination; rather, it is a question of differentiating among degrees of reciprocal determination. Expand the term *media* in this way and you get something that more plausibly "determines our situation," in the sense of material processes, such as organization, out of which those social relations emerge, and vice versa.

"Media organize" is also the thesis of *The Organizational Complex* (Martin 2003), a media history that doubles as a history of corporate architecture. There I defined the "organizational complex" emergent in the post–World War II United States as the aesthetic and technological extension of the military–industrial complex and mapped its contours at the intersection of architecture, cybernetics, and corporate sociability. *The Organizational Complex* aimed to rearrange the assumptions of my disciplinary home by arguing that architecture, understood as one among many media, evinced a feedback-oriented, modular, pattern-based "diagram" (in the Deleuzian sense, on which I will elaborate below) comparable to, but quite different from, Jeremy Bentham's much earlier panopticon. Ultimately, this diagram belonged to the affective "societies of control" that Gilles Deleuze argued had, by mid-century, begun to displace the disciplinary societies studied by Michel Foucault (Deleuze 1995).

Terminology like this is common in "new materialist" thought that speaks, as I also do, of Foucaldian *dispositifs* or apparatuses. In a more Deleuzo-Guattarian vein, such thought might contrast hierarchical treelike organizational patterns with less hierarchical rhizomelike ones. But organization is more than just a question of vertically oriented trees versus horizontally oriented rhizomes. Nor does it merely entail, to continue in the Deleuzo-Guattarian idiom, a sociospatial typology that runs from "smooth" (gaseous or fluid) to "striated" (geomorphic or crystalline). To make deeper sense of the verb *to organize,* and to get closer to the "material" of materialism by examining critically the premise of a material substrate to the social order, I want to return to certain concepts that Deleuze and Guattari elaborated by way of two instances of what is sometimes called "immaterial production."[1] One of these is a precursor to the mid-twentieth-century organizational complex; the other is among its descendants.

The first of these instances involves a contribution made by the early nineteenth-century residential college to the birth of corporate personhood, wherein the corporation becomes an entity

capable of eliciting human emotions. The second, which I will
summarize with a brief literary exposé prefaced by a theoretical
excursus, derives from the first. It involves the circulation of affect
as both capital and interpersonal social bond within a neoliberal
media complex, the diagram for which is less treelike or rhizomatic
than it is circular. Though separated by two centuries, both of these
instances refer to persons, whether corporate or individual, as
organized bodies. In arguing that media organize, then, I am more
specifically arguing that media organize *bodies*—discursive bodies,
institutional bodies, social bodies, political bodies, and biological
bodies. That is, they bind persons together, inside and out.

Persons

To begin with, recall that when Gilles Deleuze and Félix Guattari
(1987, 158) wrote of a "body without organs," they were quite specific: "The BwO is opposed not to the organs but to the organization
of the organs called the organism." The organism is what happens
when the body enters the field of power, or what Deleuze and
Guattari call, after Antonin Artaud, the "judgment of God." From
the perspective of the organizational complex, it is not accidental
that the date of Artaud's pronouncement "to have done with the
judgment of God"—November 28, 1947, which titles the relevant
chapter of *A Thousand Plateaus*—is exactly coincident with the date,
November 1947, with which Norbert Wiener (1948, 39) signed the
introduction to his book *Cybernetics; or, Control and Communication
in the Animal and the Machine,* while a visiting faculty member at
the National Institute of Cardiology in Mexico City. For, as Wiener's
institutional affiliation attests, cybernetics is nothing if not devoted
to recovering the organism as its object of cognition, at the very
moment that electromechanical technics threatened that object
with dissolution.

Recall also that in that introduction, Wiener (1948, 18) defined organization negentropically, as follows: "Just as the amount of information in a system is a measure of its degree of organization, so the
entropy of a system is a measure of its degree of disorganization;

and the one is simply the negative of the other." Encouraged at the Macy Cybernetics Conferences by Gregory Bateson and Margaret Mead to extend this principle into the domain of social organization, Wiener conceded that "it is certainly true that the social system is an organization like the individual, that it is bound together by a system of communication, and that it has a dynamics in which circular processes of a feedback nature play an important part" (24). Still, he argued that available statistical runs pertaining to human affairs were insufficiently long and insufficiently constant to obtain reliable results. This and other limitations, however, could be overcome, or at least overlooked, and within a decade, the social sciences had absorbed the cybernetic hypothesis.

Behind this well-known story is a theory of organized social life that bears closer scrutiny. In 1947, Wiener indicated his sympathy for those like Bateson and Mead who, in "the present age of confusion," sought a cybernetic social science (Wiener 1948, 33). Several years later, he attempted as much himself in his beautifully titled ramble *The Human Use of Human Beings: Cybernetics and Society* (Wiener [1950] 1954). To the extent that this later book has a focus, it is on the negentropic, homeostatic function of cybernetic feedback systems. Among its most lucid passages is a chapter added to the second edition devoted to "organization as the message," which observes that

> we have already seen that certain organisms, such as man, tend for a time to maintain and often even to increase the level of their organization, as a local enclave in the general stream of increasing entropy, of increasing chaos and de-differentiation. Life is an island here and now in a dying world. The process by which we living beings resist the general stream of corruption and decay is known as homeostasis. (95)

Wiener extrapolates a pattern-based, informational type of homeostasis ("organization as the message") from a biological one, comparing the biochemical maintenance of body temperature with the negative feedback devices of mechanical automata. It is not bodily tissue per se but "the pattern [i.e., the organism, in the Deleuzo-Guattarian sense] maintained by this homeostasis which is the touchstone of our personal identity. . . . We are but whirlpools in a river of ever-flowing water. We are not stuff that abides, but patterns that perpetuate themselves" (96). Human beings and their societies are therefore, according to Wiener, transmissable messages borne on an ever-changing material substrate that tends toward entropy. The problem in translating cybernetics to the social sciences becomes one of converting the science of neuronal or electromechanical feedback into one of pattern maintenance based on statistical data (and computing capacity) adequate to the organizational complexities of large collective bodies conceived as homeostatic organisms. But if another name for "pattern" here is not just "body" but "subject," how are such patterns produced and maintained at the sociotechnical level, that is, at the level of media complexes?

We can almost still hear Artaud shouting in protest against the organismic subject whose authority short-circuits the underlying libidinal economy circa 1947, quoted by Deleuze and Guattari (1987, 571):

> When you will have made him a body without organs then you will have delivered him from all his automatic reactions and restored him to his true freedom.

Deleuze and Guattari's version of Artaud's body-without-organs (BwO) is hence neither organic nor inorganic but rather, as they say, anorganic. That is, the BwO is not exactly a disorganized, disorderly, or anarchic body; rather, it is a form of embodied subjectivity that experiments on itself, putting itself at risk to become hypochondriac, paranoid, schizo, drugged, or masochist. The theorists quote Artaud: "*The body is the body. Alone it stands. And in no need of organs. Organism it never is. Organisms are the enemy of the body*" (158, emphasis original). Repeating the title of Artaud's radio play, they add, "The *judgment of God,* the system of the judgment of God, the theological system, is precisely the operation of He who makes an organism, an organization of organs called the organism" (158–59). Organization and stratification, then, as primordial violence, the "judgment of God": "The BwO is that glacial reality where the alluvions, sedimentations, coagulations, foldings, and recoilings that compose an organism—and also a signification and a subject—occur" (159). In short, the BwO is Norbert Wiener's "river of ever-flowing water" from which patterned organisms arise.

As "glacial reality," the BwO is not a medium. Like background noise in a communications channel, it is constitutively premedial, if by "media" we mean any apparatus that organizes this noise into "alluvions, sedimentations, coagulations, foldings, and recoilings." Here I deliberately use the Foucauldian term *apparatus* (or *dispositif*) to be more precise about defining media not as communication systems but as organizational ones, in order to address from a media-theoretical point of view and in a highly attenuated fashion the emergence of the modern corporation as a political body— that is, as an organized body, a system subject to "the judgment of God."

Among the precursors to the latter-day corporations that would consolidate a cybernetic hegemony in the neoliberal world order, and especially what is known as the Google–Apple–Facebook– Amazon (GAFA) circle, are the research universities that developed and circulated the technoscientific knowledge out of and around which that hegemony was built. In the United States in particular, many of these universities grew out of older residential colleges founded under one of several Protestant denominations and therefore subject quite directly to "the judgment of God." As colleges became universities, the "Protestant ethic" by which they were governed was secularized, or so it is still often said, with the institutionalization of the scientific method, the authority of number and calculability, the rise of vocational training, and the delinking of the humanities and the social sciences from the explicitly moral program of the church.

By the 1920s, research universities seemed to be following the pattern of "incorporation" established by the great industrial concerns—railroads, mining conglomerates, auto manufacturers— by becoming multiheaded bureaucracies. The result was the abstraction and compartmentalization of knowledge into academic departments, specialties, and subspecialties, such that by 1947, Norbert Wiener could exclaim of his colleagues, "A man may be a topologist or an acoustician or a coleopterist. He will be filled with the jargon of his field, and will know all its literature and all its ramifications, but, more frequently than not, he will regard the next subject as belonging to his colleague three doors down the corridor, and will consider any interest in it on his own part as an unwarrantable breach of privacy" (Wiener 1948, 8). Hence Wiener argued for the interdisciplinary science of cybernetics on the basis of its institutional as well as moral necessity, and with these (despite his personal misgivings), integration into a sociotechnical organism that, by 1970, was renamed the military–industrial– academic complex.

What this teleology leaves aside, however, is not only the fact that the small denominational colleges were themselves among the na- tion's earliest corporations but also the news that, as Deleuze put it in 1990, businesses—that is, corporations—had souls (Deleuze [1990] 1995, 181). Contrary to the neo-Weberian thesis and closer to the premises of the Turing test, where machine intelligence is measured by a human being's inability to distinguish a machine's communications from those of a person, corporations were like computing machines precisely to the extent that they acquired liberal human attributes, such as rights. These attributes, in turn, encouraged humans to regard the corporate body as a special kind of person, in a two-way street of subjectification that ultimately compels us to ask, what kind of human can love a corporation?

By 1800, in the early American republic, business, educational, and religious corporations were regularly formed to enable collective action like building roads or establishing cities semi-independently from the national state, which was (as now) viewed by many with suspicion. Hence the decades immediately following U.S. independence saw the proliferating incorporation of towns, turnpike authorities, bridge companies, religious associations, colleges, schools, and many other institutions. During the long nineteenth century, these corporations shifted from being conceived under the law as mere vehicles for collective activity to being recognized as active agents with rights and responsibilities of their own. The basis of this agency is what is commonly called the "legal fiction" of corporate personhood.[2]

Corporate personhood gained formal recognition in 1886 when, in *Santa Clara County v. Southern Pacific Railroad Co.,* the U.S. Supreme Court ruled that corporations were entitled to equal protection under the law as provided to natural persons under the Fourteenth Amendment, which had been ratified in 1868 largely to secure equal treatment for freed slaves. This historical irony was reaffirmed when, in 1910, the Court concluded in *Southern Railway Co. v. Greene,* "That a corporation is a person, within the meaning of the Fourteenth Amendment, is no longer open to discussion."[3] Not long thereafter, in 1926, no less a figure than John Dewey theorized "corporate personality" as, essentially, a concrete performative. Legal historians have supplied partial explanations as to how this came about, but most of these presuppose (contrary to Dewey) an ontological distinction between natural and artificial persons that is abrogated by force of law and hence construe corporate personhood as a species of literary personification.[4] This is probably because nearly all such accounts are purely discursive, giving little sense of how the corporate person was or is materially constituted.

The residential college offers early entry into that process through the 1819 U.S. Supreme Court case known as *Trustees of Dartmouth College v. Woodward,* in which the Court ruled that privately chartered institutions held contract rights comparable to those of private persons. Dartmouth College had been incorporated in 1769 by means of a charter granted by Britain's King George III, as was typical at the time (Maier 1993, 56–57).[5] Although its initial, largely unfulfilled purpose was to Christianize Indigenous youths, the precariously founded new college was, like nearly all of its peers, actually devoted to the education of white Protestant men. In 1816, in the aftermath of a conflict between the college's president and trustees, the State of New Hampshire sought to revise Dartmouth's charter to place it under the administrative control of state government. The trustees objected, arguing that this violated the contract clause of the U.S. Constitution, which prevents the state from impairing the "Obligations of Contracts" among private individuals or among individuals and the state. The Court found that the charter amounted to such a contract and that the actions of the state were in violation of this constitutional clause.[6]

But if the U.S. Supreme Court thereby recognized the already incorporated Dartmouth College as bearing the contract rights of a private individual, the means by which that recognition was secured suggest that it entailed more than just a legal fiction. In his closing argument before the Court on behalf of Dartmouth College, the orator, attorney, and Dartmouth alumnus Daniel Webster exclaimed of his alma mater to the presiding justice, John Marshall, that it is "a small college. And yet *there are those who love it.*" At which point Webster reportedly choked up, tears filling his eyes (Shewmaker 1990, 168–69, emphasis original). Strategically successful as it was, we can regard Webster's declaration of filial love for his college as genuine, not because its apparent spontaneity testified to true feeling rather than calculation, but because, as the Court's decision bore out, the college had already become a body capable of eliciting human emotion.

The evidence for this at Dartmouth and the other early colleges is abundant but counterintuitive. By the time Daniel Chester French installed his sculpture of the goddess Athena on the steps of the new Columbia University campus in 1904, refiguring her as a proud but nurturing mother, it was unproblematic—expected, even—to declare not only loyalty to but love for one's alma mater. In Foucault's language, this too was discipline. Not only did it extrapolate the maternal domestic function, during the Romantic and early Victorian periods, of training into literacy (what Friedrich Kittler mischievously called the "mother's mouth"), and not only did it extend the residential college's long-standing practice of in loco parentis into the whole university system, most importantly, it tolerated misbehavior, failure, and even delinquency, asking in return—demanding, really—only to be loved.

Remember that, as Foucault emphasizes, delinquency is a product of the carceral apparatus rather than its antithesis; failure is therefore among that apparatus's prerequisites for proper functioning. In the sphere of education, a principal instrument for the distribution of failure is the examination, the inaugural instance of which is the entrance examination. Upon arriving in Hanover, New Hampshire, in 1797, the fifteen-year-old Daniel Webster therefore had his knowledge of English, Greek, Latin, and arithmetic tested before being allowed to enroll at Dartmouth (Remini 1997, 44). Such on-the-spot exams were common at the time, as was delinquent behavior once admitted. At Princeton (then the College of New Jersey), for example, Nassau Hall, the main building, which dates from the late eighteenth century, had all the trappings of a good disciplinary apparatus (Foucault 1995, 141–54): enclosure, or confinement; a system of cellular partitioning; distinctly marked "functional sites"; and "ranks," both within rooms (rows of beds or desks) and among them (by year, etc.)—likewise class schedules; daily recitations; the teaching of proper handwriting, with proper posture; a student–pen–paper–chair–desk interface; and various prohibitions on time wasting, etc. More than simply a building, then, Nassau Hall was a media complex. As such, it was repeatedly the object of destructive behavior.

During the 1810s, for example, three students were expelled for exploding gunpowder in the building, another for unforgivably ringing the belfry bell at 3:00 A.M., while another vandalized a Bible by cutting a deck of playing cards into its leaves, and others set off firecrackers indoors and scrawled graffiti on the walls, a sequence that reached a climax of sorts when several students exploded a gunpowder-filled log inside the hall, only to be topped three

years later by a group who nailed all the building's doors shut and
shouted "Rebellion!" and "Fire!" (Wertenbaker 1946, 156, 167).

Anyone even remotely aware of the sexualized emotions that simmer beneath the surface of collegiate life, sometimes violently, will recognize this ritual misbehavior as more than just boys testing the patience of their surrogate parents. It may indeed be that, like Artaud, these student-subjects, wanting to be "done with the judgment of God," or at least of their parents, are experimenting on the body of the college, looking for ways to defeat it, to dismember it, even to make it into a "body-without-organs." But in so doing, *they also affirm that body's personhood,* its organic-machinic subjectivity. This violence belongs to the order of "male fantasy," which, as Klaus Theweleit ([1987] 1989) showed, mixes desire, fear, hatred, and love with a will to power focused on and through the technologically produced corporate organism. In the process, that organism becomes a real subject, organized by media in the expanded sense of a material environment like the all-purpose Nassau Hall or its northern relative, Dartmouth Hall. As Daniel Webster said of Dartmouth College, the institution embodied in the building, there are necessarily "those who love it." Like the news that businesses have souls, this is enough to make us shudder.

When we say that media organize, then, and go so far as to assert that the term *media* is even defined by this organizational function, we are actually speaking of an intermediality that runs, in this case, from paper to candlelight to recitation room to courtroom, and well beyond. And if to organize is to distribute the background noise of a "glacial reality," a "river of ever-flowing water," into a nonfictional organism capable of bearing rights, being hated, and being loved, the field of practices that recognize this organism and make it into a subject runs in a highly modulated continuum from oral examination (or job interview, as the case may be) to nocturnal outburst. That field's organization—into patterns of power, knowledge, and desire—is not legible outside the ensuing interactions. Arising from all of this, the corporate person warrants our closest attention.

Machines

As I have argued, media organize social and political life, as well as the social and political imagination, through a variety of channels that extend well beyond the communicative functions traditionally ascribed to technical devices like Kittler's celebrated triumvirate of "gramophone, film, typewriter." In treating things like buildings as media, we are extending analytic techniques developed to understand these more classical media formats into areas that have analytical languages of their own. The methodological challenge, then, is to translate the one into the other without flattening either into unrecognizability. For this, an intermediary language is helpful. Therefore the following excursus continues in the Deleuzo-Guattarian idiom, in an effort to be both theoretically and descriptively specific.

Consider the term *machine.* There is a long tradition in architectural studies that treats buildings as machines. Among that tradition's most eloquent representatives is the American cultural critic Lewis Mumford, whose intellectual project was, in many respects, to secularize what he called in his later work the "myth of the machine." By this Mumford meant the metaphysical power attributed by the mid-twentieth century to mechanization, the chief example of which was the social and political order inaugurated by nuclear weaponry. The "machine," in Mumford's sense, was much more than the weaponry itself; it was the entire social and political system to which nuclear weapons belonged—the military, the corporations, the universities—a system, or in Mumford's terms a "complex," that closely resembles one of Foucault's "apparatuses."

But where do these apparatuses come from? In the chapter of *A Thousand Plateaus* immediately prior to that devoted to the "body without organs," Deleuze and Guattari address this question by rethinking semiotics in a manner that culminates in the elusive concept of the "abstract machine." An abstract machine is, in their language, something like the operating system of a corporeal "assemblage" (or sometimes a "machinic assemblage"), which we can understand as Deleuze and Guattari's answer to Foucault's sociotechnical "apparatus." In the background runs an effort to rethink communication by recasting the sign–signified relation as merely one of many possible semiotic systems, or "regimes of signs." Of these many regimes, Deleuze and Guattari (1987, 135) identify four: a "presignifying semiotic," to which they somewhat dubiously link certain premodern societies; a "signifying semiotic" centered on the signifier–signified relation, which they identify with the despotic state or the Judeo-Christian God; a "countersignifying semiotic" operated by a revolutionary nomadic "war machine"; and a "postsignifying semiotic" governed by what they call "passional" forms of subjectification. Despite appearances, these are not evolutionary stages. In the Deleuzo-Guattarian idiom, they are strata, or organizational levels, that coexist in impure mixtures in any given historical situation. Nonetheless, any given situation will favor one stratum or the other, or one particular admixture over another. Historical change entails a move from one stratum to the other through semiotic recombination or reshuffling.

Each stratum also takes a specific organizational form. Presignification is plurivocal. It proceeds along discrete segments, or pathways, in which signs do not refer to other signs but rather belong to particular ritual-lived domains where expressions do not translate from one to the other. In contrast, signification is concentric. Signs refer to other signs in a semiotic spiral, with each new ring corresponding to a new form of interpretation governed by priests, psychoanalysts, and other "despots" paranoically orbiting an empty, metaphysical center, whereas countersignification is numerical, where number does not represent or signify anything; rather, it arranges and distributes, or organizes. A countersignifying machine is like a nomadic military system distributed numerically "into tens, fifties, hundreds, thousands, etc." that aims to abolish the sedentary state but is also adopted by it. Finally, postsignification is punctual. It operates around what Deleuze and Guattari call "points of departure" that mark two forms of subjectivity, the "subject of enunciation" and the "subject of the statement," joined by a line that brings both into being. Postsignification is active rather than ideational. It is, they say, authoritarian rather than despotic, proletarian rather than bourgeois, and monomaniacal rather than paranoid, more like Franz Kafka's linear bureaucratic "proceedings" than the jurist Daniel Paul Schreber's "radiating paranoia" (117–21).

The two postsignifying subjects, of enunciation and of the statement, can be distinguished from the punctual "sender" and "addressee" of mid-century communications theory in two ways. First, they do not preexist the signifying act but rather are constituted by it. Second, from the point of view of the "abstract machine" governing the entire system, these two forms of subjectivity ultimately belong to one and the same subject, who is not so much split but doubled up into a subject that obeys its own commands.

Constantly changing places, these "points of departure" for subjectification are always multiple not only within a given society but within a given individual.[7] Hence subjects—in our opening example, corporate persons, meaning both the colleges and their students—are not just speaking subjects, determined in the legal context from which they emerged by a capacity for (or a "right" to) political speech. Like all other subjects, corporate persons arise from a constant movement from point to point and from speaker to receiver, always doubling up enunciation and statement. They speak and are spoken to at once, in an internalized feedback loop: "*The subject of enunciation recoils into the subject of the statement, to the point that the subject of the statement resupplies [a] subject of enunciation for another proceeding*" (129, emphasis original). Deleuze and Guattari refer to the line along which this process occurs as a "passional line" that originates with, or departs from, a point of subjectification, which can be anything in the world. For someone in love, for example, this point can be what they call a "faciality trait" (let's say, a building facade, or a sculpture of Alma Mater), where "faciality" no longer refers to an embodied signifier but rather acts as a trigger for—again in the Deleuzo-Guattarian idiom—"deterritorialized" associations along a "line of flight" (129).

Under the sign of corporate personhood, I am suggesting, this line ultimately becomes circular.

An assemblage governed by an abstract machine comprises both sides of this doubling. On one side is enunciation, which "formalizes expression," and on the other is the field of contents, or embodied, normalizing statements like those issued by teachers under strictly delimited speaking conditions to organize a "machinic assemblage or an assemblage of bodies" in the sense that Foucault attributes, for example, to the carceral or disciplinary apparatus. But the causal relation between the two is nonlinear; forms of content (bodies organized into/by statements) cannot be derived linearly from modes or structures of enunciation or expression. That is, students cannot be derived from teachers or teachers from students; nor can either be derived from the educational institution. Rather, teachers, students, and schools are joined in a circular abstract machine, which I have called above a "person," and which "operates by *matter,* not by substance; by *function,* not by form," by way of what Deleuze and Guattari call "a diagram independent of the forms and substances, expressions and contents it will distribute" (141). Abstract machines do not communicate, in the sense of transmitting messages or expressions; rather, "writing now functions on the same level as the real, and the real materially writes" (141).

Abstract machines, which we can still call media, are therefore neither infrastructural nor transcendental; rather, they are immanent to semiotechnics, where they play a creative "piloting role." To specify the type of abstraction they have in mind, Deleuze and Guattari add another category to the Peircean semiotic triad of indexes, icons, and symbols, which they call (again after Peirce) a "diagram." Not exactly a visual map or code, a diagram is, in this sense, more like a coherent set of techniques for, as they put it, "conjugating matter and function" (143). In the case of the corporate person, "love," in my argument, is one such technique.

Circumscribed as it may be by an idiosyncratic philosophical system, the set of concepts derived from Deleuze and Guattari's pragmatic semiotics is useful in sketching the rudiments of a media theory of organization to the extent that it expands that term's—"organization's"—referents. Among the examples with which Deleuze and Guattari conclude their revision of semiotics is a brief analysis of the proposition "I love you." They ask to what regime the proposition might belong. For us, this is principally the passional or postsignifying regime, mixed with the oedipal, patriarchal signifying or despotic regime. They ask what translations it enables. For us, as we will shortly see, it entails among others a translation with the countersignifying war machine. They ask what is its diagram, what are its abstract machines? For us, it is postpanoptic but still circular. Finally, they ask to what machinic assemblages it belongs. For us: the "megamachine" (147–48).

Still bearing in mind the example of the corporate antebellum college but now moving the genealogical needle significantly forward to the modern (and postmodern) corporation, we can understand the proposition "I love you" as harboring a set of organizational techniques that are hardly limited to those from which the set of legal–juridical statements associated with corporate personhood eventually derived. Among these techniques, the organization of subjects into bodies deserves further elaboration. Having described passional love as an intense form of intersubjective doubling, a "cogito built for two" that is also always a betrayal, a turning away of faces, Deleuze and Guattari repeatedly point out that with every opening, there is a closing. The open field of promiscuous, polysemic coupling closes down into conjugality (the nuclear family), and the polymorphous cogito becomes a bureaucracy (the office) where the bureaucrat, or we could add, the student-teacher, says "*I think*" (131–32). Impassioned declarations of love, then, are double sided. On one hand, they operate the abstract machine and the diagram—"love"—to produce new, uninhibited couplings, bodies-without-organs in which we discern remnants of the "desiring machines" of the *Anti-Oedipus*. While on the other hand, these declarations of love domesticate desire in a bureaucratic assemblage of nucleated, signifying couples mixed with a war machine.

In recent times, the name of that bureaucratic assemblage has been the state. To explain, Deleuze and Guattari borrow from Mumford, whom they summon alongside Marx to chart the longue durée of "capture," or state formation, by what Mumford calls a "megamachine." Associating what Mumford describes as the despotic "megamachines" of the ancient empires with Marx's "Asiatic" or imperial–agrarian mode of production and exchange, Deleuze and Guattari trace a genealogy of the state as a system of capture that converts territory into land, property, and credit through a series of techniques including rent, profit, and taxation (443–44). Today, the governing paradigm of capture is the corporation.

But what happens when the ruled says to the ruler, "I love you"? At first glance, this would seem the simplest of interpellations with transparently pastoral origins, wherein the ruled willingly responds to a command to submit. This, however, decodes the exclamation only at the level of the signifying regime, with its spiral of interpretations spinning around an empty, metaphysical void. "Hey, you there!" says Louis Althusser's state apparatus. You turn to face the police, thereby closing the circle and inaugurating the hermeneutic inquest: Are you a criminal? Are you hungry? Are you mad? Are you married? Whereas, on the "passional" level, state and subject trade places in the semiotic system, doubling up into temporarily unstable chimeras—Donna Haraway's ([1984] 1991) cyborgs— switching uniforms and recoding bodies. This is the level on which corporations, as organs of capture derived from and supporting the capitalist state, become persons capable of loving and being loved.

It is no accident, then, that Mumford's rage against the modern, nuclear-armed "megamachine," which threatens to recapitulate the cruelties of ancient despots with an exponentially enhanced efficiency, returns repeatedly to communications technologies. Standing opposite the ordering systems of the military–industrial complex, he argues, are Marshall McLuhan's "trancelike" predictions of "an electronic anti-megamachine programmed to accelerate disorder, ignorance, and entropy." "In revolt against totalitarian organization and enslavement," says Mumford in 1970, "the generation now responding to McLuhan's doctrines would seek total 'liberation' from organization, continuity, and purpose of any sort in systematic de-building, dissolution, and de-creation. Ironically, such a return to randomness would, according to probability theory, produce the most static and predicable state possible: that of unorganized 'matter'" (293).

All of this appears on pages referenced by Deleuze and Guattari, and we would not be wrong in noticing a relationship between what Mumford calls "unorganized matter" and the "body without organs." Recall, however, that a key attribute of the abstract machine is that it is material but insubstantial. The anorganic body (the BwO) is an intermediary operating in the no-man's land between substance and matter, form and formlessness, out of which the paranoid idealizations of absolute organization and absolute entropy spring. The diagrammatic abstract machine, which I am still calling a "person," is immanent to the sociotechnical assemblage of the megamachine without being identical with it; a pure yet always emergent functionality distinguishes this "person" from an "ideal" form or a universal axiomatic (like, say, the "human" of humanism), while its sociotechnical diffusion makes it more real than formal abstractions like "sender" or "receiver." So can there be a media theory of abstract machines? Yes, when we correlate the two poles of organization and entropy with a deterritorializing (or disorganizing) and reterritorializing (or reorganizing) movement between semiotic levels and between "apparatuses of capture," meaning regimes of power, within which diagrams become legible and operate.

Mumford (1970, 378–93) responded to the totalitarian organization of the Cold War megamachine (which he also called the "Power Complex") by calling for an "organic world picture" embodied in a "new organum." Calls like this, which in Mumford's case sought a biotechnical homeostasis understood ecologically rather than mechanically, were a commonplace of the "new humanism" that dominated antitechnocratic thought during the mid-century, of which Mumford's, like Norbert Wiener's, was a representative voice. What he, Wiener, and many of their contemporaries missed, however, was that, in posing as a form of organized life—in Mumford's case, decentralized, face-to-face, communal—that escaped both the rigid, institutional powers of the military–industrial complex and the entropy of a technophilic counterculture, this humanist organicism (what Wiener called "the human use of human beings") belonged to a new machinic assemblage and a new diagram of power in its own right: the corporation-as-person and the person-as-corporation.

We can call this diagram "organizational" in a sense that translates the paranoid, modular signifying systems of an indifferent "megamachine" into the intimate, "passional" domain of corporate personhood with which we began. Mumford encapsulates the long-term transition between what Deleuze and Guattari call "apparatuses of capture" with a comparison between the Egyptian sun god, Re, and the modern megamachine, or as his subtitle calls it, the "Pentagon of Power." What the sun god enunciates with sublime monuments, the modern state insinuates:

> In more devious symbolic ways these same awe-inspiring creatures still stand at the portals of the Power Pentagon today, though the god they represent, whose secret knowledge cannot be challenged and whose divine commands cannot be questioned, turns out actually to be, when one tears aside the curtain, only the latest model IBM computer, zealously programmed by Dr. Strangelove and his assistants. (Mumford 1970, 403)

Perhaps, however, in his eagerness to decode Dr. Strangeglove as a sign of the times, Mumford forgot the ironic subtitle of Stanley Kubrick's 1964 antinuclear send-up: "How I Learned to Stop Worrying and Love the Bomb." What the film satirizes as willing interpellation into the megamachine's logic of "mutually assured destruction" (MAD) was, in fact, its means of production: if not exactly love, then recognition, as in a mirror.

The Cold War megamachine is a bureaucracy piloted by what we might call, in a Deleuzo-Guattarian manner, a "Strangeglove abstract machine." In such a machine, both syntagmatically and paradigmatically, the "I" that loves "the bomb" is the conjugal and bureaucratic double of the organizational complex, in whom a passion for the self as a thinking–feeling subject (as consumer and as corporation) combines with family values and corporate conformism. On the conjugal–bureaucratic normalization of passional love, Deleuze and Guattari write (1987, 132),

> Conjugality is the development of the couple, and bureaucracy is the development of the cogito. But one is contained in the other: amorous bureaucracy, bureaucratic couple. Too much has been written on the double, haphazardly, metaphysically, finding it everywhere, in any old mirror, without noticing the specific regime it possesses both in a mixed semiotic where it introduces new phases, and in the pure semiotic of subjectification where it inscribes itself on a line of flight and introduces very particular figures.

But where, they argue, at the level of the signifying regime, these kinds of redundancies are most often described in terms of frequency (of signifier–signified, sign–sign relations), in the post-signifying or passional regime of subjectification, redundancy is a form of resonance, an echo, which transmediates mirror-optics into audio-acoustics (132–33). Thus, on the order of signification, in learning to "love" the megamachine, the organized corporate subject recognizes herself in the blankness of its reflective surfaces. While on the order of subjectification, megamachine and corporate subject bring one another into being along a resonant, passional "line of flight" distantly descended from the orator Daniel Webster's impassioned voice arguing for corporate rights before the Supreme Court: "And yet *there are those who love it*."

An emergent sovereign—the corporate "person," as individual and as group—whose organic, organized body reterritorializes

the whole affair, blocks escape along this line. In a manner related
to what the medievalist Ernst Kantorowicz described as the
"king's two bodies," the new sovereign's body is also doubled up,
comprising on one hand living organs, in the bodies of its mortal
human constituents and their sociotechnical apparatuses, and on
the other a seemingly immortal being, the bureaucratic cogito (in-
terpellated by the old IBM command: "Think"), whose life extends
beyond that of any individual. Rather than remaining trapped,
then, in a prison house of language or of concentric signifiers, as
in Bentham's panopticon, the prisoner, subject of the conjugal
family and of the office bureaucracy out of which the "bomb" was
born, builds a postpanoptic prison even as she is built by it, in a
recursive process for which the Deleuzian term *assemblage,* with
its echoes of the linear, mechanistic "assembly line," is not entirely
adequate. The term *complex* brings us closer, with its evocation
of nonlinear networks and feedback loops. More literal still is the
circle, which echoes in the mixed semiotic of the megamachine
the redundant despotisms of signification spinning around
an empty center (Artaud's "judgment of God," Strangeglove's
paranoia), but actually comprises an amorous, feedback-based
network: a network of circles. Of this, a brief concluding example
must suffice.

Circles

The most complete corporate body is circular. Today, both
sociologists and entrepreneurs might describe what are known
colloquially as "social circles" or "circles of friends" as networks, to
emphasize the interconnectedness of their members as well as
their seemingly inherent incompleteness and open-endedness.
Organization, in this language, is pattern based in the sense that
it entails the networked formation of social bodies, with different
degrees and types of hierarchy, and different mechanisms of inclu-
sion and exclusion. But it may well be that the older colloquialism,
"social circles," captures something that the newer one, "social
networks," leaves out.

When, to assist fellow college students in recognizing one another on campus and, we can infer, as future alumni bound filially and financially to Alma Mater, more recent subjects of the megamachinic complex converted printed college "facebooks" into an online platform, they conjugated the bureaucratic coupling of love and (re)cognition already present on campus under a watchful motherly gaze, into a new and properly circular being: the individual as a corporate person. This being's diagram is satirized, incompletely, in Dave Eggers's (2013) novel of passional, tech-campus subjectification, *The Circle.* The obvious architectural reference (and Bentham equivalent) is not Facebook but rather the new Apple campus designed by the architect Norman Foster in Cupertino, California, as an enormous circular extrusion, with a minimalist, streamlined shell; a pleasantly empty, landscaped center; and a more or less continuous 1970s-style "office landscape" *(Bureaulandschaft)* interior. In Eggers's novel, the narrative turns on the project of "closing" the Circle (the name of the corporation in question) by incorporating all of humanity into its networks, a quest led by an improbably earnest protagonist who begins her employment as a customer service representative at what amounts to an on-campus call center. Following a familiar Silicon Valley pattern, the corporation's forever-new office complex grows rapidly into something resembling a residential college campus, with a full suite of leisure activities, medical services, and dormitories to complement the open work areas where "Circlers" communicate with one another and with their clients. Insubordination of the nineteenth-century sort is unheard of.

A central technique for achieving corporate closure is the customer survey, which plays a role comparable to that of the examination, the classic disciplinary instrument of educational institutions. In a parody of the social media system of ratings and reviews, Eggers portrays the quest for ever higher customer satisfaction as a form of recruitment into the social circles of the corporation. Employees, who are acutely aware of their various scores (including one for participation in on-campus after-hours social programs), build ever-growing concentric relationships of sympathy, admiration, support, and—yes—love with customers who appear principally as names and addresses rather than faces. The technical systems including the buildings and the personnel that enable all of this are necessary but not sufficient for the organization, or, in Mumford's terms, the social organism, to survive and thrive. There must also be something like an abstract machine—let us call it a "love" machine—that all of these processes operate materially. If its diagram, like that of Bentham's panopticon, is circular, it is in a decentered rather than a centered sense, for in the Circle we are principally in Deleuze and Guattari's postsignifying regime. Where Bentham's concentric prison retained a ghostly, godlike referent at its voided center, Foster's (and Eggers's) circular form, like the data gathered by and about the Circlers, "means" nothing, nor does it ask us to decode its nonexistent semantics. In the novel, nearly ubiquitous, miniaturized audiovisual surveillance does play its part in eliciting social performances from customers that draw them further in, but it is a form of surveillance—and mutual recognition—in which everyone is watching everyone else without hierarchies of the teacher–student, parent–child, employer–employee, warden–prisoner variety. Rather, only relations of inside and outside obtain. Either you are inside the circle or you are not.

Eggers, who appears uncomfortable with satire, limits his critique to one close to Mumford's: behind the Circle is a machine that distorts human relations into numerical ones. But lest we forget, the Circle is, like Apple, Facebook, and all the rest, a person. I deliberately do not enclose that term in scare quotes ("person") to emphasize the reality of the abstraction. Neither in the novel nor in the film based on it do we find much evidence of the organon, or curriculum, from which the Circle might have derived when we remember its origins on the college campus. What we see instead is an evacuation of that curriculum, in the traditional sense of a medium of *Bildung,* or of personal growth, in favor of sheer face-to-face-to-face-to-face communication among subjects of enunciation-without-statements, content-free expressions of pure recognition that, pace Mumford, do not tend toward entropy but rather toward tautological, circular organization. For the *person* is the real name for the diagram and the abstract machine that the modern corporation operates, as an institution that demands, with grim determination, our deepest affection, if not our undying love.

And yet, visible evidence of the military–security megamachine is mostly absent from *The Circle.* In its place are needy, vacant, rebellious consumer-humans, embodied parodies of the counter-culture (Turner 2006). At one level, the elision is straightforwardly ideological; the very term *social media* masks the historical relation, traceable to Norbert Wiener's early servomechanisms, between feedback and targeting. Where there are targets, whether of missiles or of marketing, there are commanders ready to issue the command: "Fire!" In Silicon Valley as elsewhere, these commanders remain in abundant supply. But a media theory that considers only them remains a theory of signification devoted principally to demystifying the "judgment of God." To touch what Deleuze and Guattari awkwardly call the "postsignifying" level, or better, the "passional" level, we must learn to see the circle itself as an embod-ied, sovereign being doubled up in the bodies of its subjects. In that sense, the organic social body incorporated by social media *is* the megamachine.

So yes, media organize. This does not mean that all forms of or-ganization, networked or otherwise, tend toward domination. On the contrary, media enable solidarities of all kinds. Nor does the genealogy of corporate affection I have sketched herein simply and irresponsibly replace human agency with an allegedly impersonal system, or complex. Rather, my effort has been to recognize how, over time, that system has been personalized in a practical, per-formative sense. To replace the deadly megamachine with other, more just forms of collective life requires breaking the circle of corporate personhood. Among other things, this means unlearning how to love the bomb by refusing that circle's disarmingly friendly, and sometimes amorous, advances.

But it also means learning to live with the ruins of past solidarities
and their institutional forms while affirming their ghostly per-
sistence. If my historical argument has suggested anything, it is that
when it comes to the incorporation of subjects, our newest media
forms or platforms are not entirely new. This perspective restates
the problem as one of confronting what persists as well as what
changes, both materially and conceptually. To conclude with another, seemingly incongruous architectural example: in the Circle,
the most dedicated employees live on campus, in dormitories. An
important counterpoint (but also silent partner) to the corporate
organizational matrices of the 1950s and 1960s were the massive
social housing programs associated with the welfare state and
with state socialism, begun in the 1920s and continued around the
world until about 1970. Their dismantling, often accompanied by
spectacular, mass-mediated demolitions, is one of the hallmarks of
the neoliberal era. The response on the Left has been ambivalent.
On one hand, these "projects" were avatars of economic redistri-
bution and, sometimes, of genuine collectivism; equally, however,
they were the biopolitical instruments of paternalistic, racist, and
imperialist state bureaucracies. Hence, in a signal instance of
performative incommunicability, summoning their ghosts in an
affirmative, nonnostalgic fashion has proved exceptionally difficult,
if not impossible.

Can the question of organization, then, critically posed, be redirect-
ed away from claustrophobic corporate feedback loops and toward
concerns as prosaic—and, dare I say, as universal—as housing?
Rephrasing the housing question in this manner is well beyond the
scope of what I have attempted here. I refer to it only to concretize
the implications and open the frame of reference. Follow any
network and you find that its edges fray. There, illuminated by the
fluorescent light of history, the outside occasionally enters in.

Notes

With gratitude to Timon Beyes, Lisa Conrad, Götz Bachmann, Ned Rossiter, and
Geert Lovink for their thoughtful responses to this text.

1   On "immaterial production," see, e.g., Hardt and Negri (2009, 132–33).

2   The following discussion of colleges and corporate personhood is adapted from my more detailed "Corporate Personhood: Notes toward an Architectural Genealogy" (Martin 2017). On the political and legal history of corporate personhood, see Maier (1993) and Winkler (2018).

3   Southern Railway Co. v. Greene, 216 U.S. 400 (1910), http://caselaw.findlaw .com/us-supreme-court/216/400.html. For a summary of this history, see Barkan (2013) and Sklar (1988, 49–53).

4   Barkan refuses this distinction, arguing instead that corporate personhood constitutes a *dispositif* or apparatus critical to "corporate sovereignty," which, like the *dispositif* of the "person" more generally, as theorized by the philosopher Roberto Esposito after Giorgio Agamben, operates a "ban" whereby the corporate entity is granted exceptional legal status or rights in the name, paradoxically, of fulfilling its societal obligations under the law (Barkan 2013, 76–86). On legal personhood as a concrete performative, see Dewey (1926).

5   On the history of the corporate charter, see Handlin and Handlin (1945).

6   For a detailed study of the Dartmouth case, see Stites (1972). The "contracts clause" is to be found in article I, section 10 of the U.S. Constitution.

7   As Deleuze and Guattari put it (1987, 129), "the various forms of education or 'normalization' imposed upon an individual consist in making him or her change points of subjectification, always moving toward a higher, nobler one in closer conformity with the supposed ideal. Then from the point of subjectification issues a subject of enunciation, as a function of mental reality determined by that point. Then from that subject of enunciation issues a subject of the statement, in other words, a subject bound to statements in conformity with a dominant reality (of which the mental reality just mentioned is a part, even when it seems to oppose it)."

References

Barkan, Joshua. 2013. *Corporate Sovereignty: Law and Government under Capitalism.* Minneapolis: University of Minnesota Press.

Deleuze, Gilles. (1990) 1995. "Postscript on Control Societies." In *Negotiations 1972– 1990,* translated by Martin Joughin, 177–82. New York: Columbia University Press.

Deleuze, Gilles, and Félix Guattari. 1987. *A Thousand Plateaus: Capitalism and Schizophrenia.* Translated by Brian Massumi. Minneapolis: University of Minnesota Press.

Dewey, John. 1926. "The Historic Background of Corporate Legal Personality." *Yale Law Journal* 35, no. 6: 655–73.

Eggers, Dave. 2013. *The Circle: A Novel.* New York: Alfred A. Knopf.

Foucault, Michel. 1995. *Discipline and Punish: The Birth of the Prison.* Translated by Alan Sheridan. New York: Vintage Books.

Handlin, Oscar, and Mary F. Handlin. 1945. "Origins of the American Business Corporation." *Journal of Economic History* 5, no. 1: 1–23.

Haraway, Donna J. (1984) 1991. "A Cyborg Manifesto: Science, Technology, and

Socialist-Feminism in the Late Twentieth Century." In *Simians, Cyborgs, and Women:* **27**
The Reinvention of Nature. New York: Routledge.

Hardt, Michael, and Antonio Negri. 2009. *Commonwealth.* Cambridge, Mass.: Harvard
University Press.

Kittler, Friedrich A. 1986. *Gramophone, Film, Typewriter.* Translated by Geoffrey
Winthrop-Young and Michael Wutz. Stanford, Calif.: Stanford University Press.

Maier, Pauline. 1993. "The Revolutionary Origins of the American Corporation."
William and Mary Quarterly 50, no. 1: 53–58.

Martin, Reinhold. 2003. *The Organizational Complex: Architecture, Media, and Corporate
Space.* Cambridge, Mass.: MIT Press.

Martin, Reinhold. 2017. "Corporate Personhood: Notes toward an Architectural Genealogy." In *Architecture/Machine: Programs, Processes, and Performances,* edited by
Laurent Stalder and Moritz Gleich, 28–37. Zurich: gta Verlag, ETH Zurich.

Mumford, Lewis. 1970. *The Myth of the Machine: The Pentagon of Power.* New York:
Harcourt Brace Jovanovich.

Remini, Robert V. 1997. *Daniel Webster: The Man and His Time.* New York: W. W. Norton.

Shewmaker, Kenneth E., ed. 1990. *Daniel Webster, "the Completest Man": Documents
from the Daniel Webster Papers.* Hanover, N.H.: Dartmouth College/University
Press.

Sklar, Martin J. 1988. *The Corporate Reconstruction of American Capitalism, 1890–1916:
The Market, the Law, and Politics.* New York: Cambridge University Press.

Stites, Francis N. 1972. *Private Interest and Public Gain: The Dartmouth College Case,
1819.* Amherst: University of Massachusetts Press.

Theweleit, Klaus. (1987) 1989. *Male Fantasies.* 2 vols. Translated by Stephen Conway.
Minneapolis: University of Minnesota Press.

Turner, Fred. 2006. *From Counterculture to Cyberculture: Stewart Brand, the Whole Earth
Network, and the Rise of Digital Utopianism.* Chicago: University of Chicago Press.

Wertenbaker, Thomas Jefferson. 1946. *Princeton, 1746–1896.* Princeton, N.J.: Princeton
University Press.

Wiener, Norbert. 1948. *Cybernetics; or, Control and Communication in the Animal and
the Machine.* Cambridge, Mass.: Technology Press/John Wiley.

Wiener, Norbert. (1950) 1954. *The Human Use of Human Beings: Cybernetics and Society.* New York: Doubleday.

Winkler, Adam. 2018. *We the Corporations: How American Businesses Won Their Civil
Rights.* New York: Liveright.

2

Organizing Media: Security and Entertainment

Timon Beyes

Orgware

One of the most remarkable works on display at 2015's Venice
Biennale in Italy was Simon Denny's installation *Secret Power.* Con-
cocted with the designer David Bennewith, the exhibition staged an
artistic inquiry into how the world is imagined, mapped, and organized according to the National Security Agency (NSA) and its "Five
Eyes" allies, the intelligence apparatuses of the United Kingdom,
Australia, Canada, and New Zealand. Representing New Zealand
in the Biennale's exhausting mix of centrally curated show and
dozens of national pavilions, *Secret Power*'s main location was the
time-honored Biblioteca Nazionale Marciana, a library representing
Venice as an affluent and influential world power during the Renaissance. Completed in 1588, the Renaissance Biblioteca had been
built in an era of expansionism, empire, and early globalization.
It was designed to celebrate culture, knowledge, and science in
harmony with civil and military duties and, of course, the church.
Its walls are adorned with paintings by then-famous artists (Titian,
Tintoretto, and Veronese among them), depicting philosophers
and thinkers, and its ceilings with allegorical images about the

organization of knowledge and power as enacted by the organizational apparatuses of state, military, and church. In the early seventeenth century, the Venetian authorities decreed that a copy of each and every new publication would need to be deposited in the library. Celebrating the medium of the book and of maps—among them Fra Mauro's *Map of the World* from circa 1450, which summarizes the cartographic thought of its time—in 2015, the library's walls and ceilings serve as iconographic backdrop and correspondence to *Secret Power.*

Denny and Bennewith have turned the library into a contemporary server room. In an infrastructural double of hardware and exhibition architecture, the visitor encounters an ensemble of nine half-empty server racks—in Plexiglas enclosures that simultaneously work as vitrines—and a workstation. Moving from vitrine to vitrine perhaps echoes the practice of browsing from one internet window to the next (Gad 2015, 188). The blinking hard drives integrated into the racks are apparently at work, processing data and generating information that the visitors cannot access; one has to make do with what is made visible to the human eye. Roughly one-half of the "server vitrines" focus on a montage and sculptural interpretations of selected sets of slides and documents

[Figure 2.1]. Simon Denny, *Secret Power,* installation view, Marciana Library, 2015. Photograph by Jens Ziehe.

leaked by Edward Snowden. Vis-à-vis, the other half of the vitrines is stranger still. The objects on display are based on the portfolio of a designer and entrepreneur by the name of David Darchicourt, whose social media profile states that he was the NSA's creative director of defense intelligence from 2001 to 2012. The material visually resembles the NSA infographics, tools, and plans as well as other material leaked by Snowden. Yet it seems to (at least mainly) consist of Darchicourt's own work as well as sculptural reinterpretations of his designs.

Nothing here seems made up or invented by the artist. Presenting a "mimesis of the given" (Foster 2017, 78), most of the material was found on the internet, then partly processed and remediated, synthesized and collated, by the artist. The rendering of the material is on one hand forensic, evidence exhibited and magnified. Yet the connections and juxtapositions seem impressionistic and circumstantial, conjectural and speculative (Leonard 2015). There is an obvious allegorical layer, given the juxtaposition of contemporary "secret power" and the historical depictions (of power and knowledge) on the library's walls and ceiling. At the same time, the installation's atmosphere is brash and vulgar, since the presentation of the material relies strongly on commercial printing and prototyping techniques, perhaps harking back to the *Wunderkammer* aesthetics of early museums and libraries (Byrt 2016). Overall, it seems more trade fair than art space—as if an ethnographic museum would try to present the workings of intelligence agencies.[1]

Forensic and allegorical, ethnographic and speculative: what is at stake in the exhibition, and what it enables the viewer to register and think, goes beyond the staging of an intelligence agency's visual culture. On display are organizational documents and machines, symbols and traces, agents and structures: the installation is largely made up of *orgware.* It is "speaking of organization in its own language" (Latour 2013a, 381). Yet, in suggesting conjectures and connections between these materials, and in relation to the allegorical depictions of the organization of power/knowledge that adorn the library's walls and ceiling, the exhibition goes further than speaking of organization in its own language. It seems to speculatively trace a contemporary constellation of sociotechnical ordering and its effects. This constellation or nexus operates both technologically and aesthetically: it relies on media infrastructures and networks, and it shapes what can be experienced and expressed. This way, *Secret Power* not only makes manifest what might be the most elaborated and wide-ranging surveillance system ever imagined (Byrt 2016); it also presents a troubling interdependence of technologically driven forms of organizing and conjures up an organizational nexus that coalesces around modes of algorithmic and affective, bureaucratic and entrepreneurial, ordering.

Thinking Organizationally

The Berlin-based and New Zealand–born Denny has been called a "post-internet artist" (Leonard 2015, 11). His work suits the notion of a "postdigital aesthetics" in that it takes pervasive digitization of everyday life, global networking of communication, "and the immersive and disorientating experiences of computational infrastructures" for granted (Berry and Dieter 2015, 5). Schooled in conceptualism, pop art, and minimalism, and working with all sorts of artistic media, the artist investigates and makes present the images, rhetorics, and mechanisms—or perhaps the visual clutter, rhetorical noise, and hidden operations—of an organized world shaped by pervasive and ubiquitous computing. According to writer and art critic Chris Kraus (2015, 20), Denny therefore engages in a kind of anthropology of contemporary media culture. He identifies aspects of this culture and then transplants and remediates them into the bracketed spaces of museums and galleries—perhaps a translation of the legacy of ready-made sculptures into a postdigital world (Byrt 2016).

Denny's particular focus is on the digital economy, and he makes no secret of his infatuation with tech culture as it materializes in, and is driven by, businesses and start-ups.[2] In its emphasis on organizational contexts, then, his work manifests a kind of artistic–

organizational research. An anthropologist's eye is turned to the
aesthetics of organization that shape, and that are shaped by, the
age of ubiquitous computing and connectivity "after" digital media.
In this sense, these installations present investigations of "organization" and "organizing" as decisive phenomena of the contemporary
media-technological situation. They interrogate and stage how
"media organize" (Martin 2003, 15), how media are organized, and
how organizing is mediated. They therefore perform a seemingly
simple yet consequential recursive logic: to explore how media
technologies condition contemporary life, one needs to inquire into
their organizational effects. And to discuss how media technologies
are produced, take place, disappear, or are transformed, one
needs to trace the organizational constellations in which they are
inscribed and which they make possible.[3]

Adopting Bruno Latour's plea for the deployment of adverbial
forms to understand organization as a "mode of existence" (Latour
2013b), Denny's work can thus be understood as an art of thinking
and speaking organizationally. Thinking and speaking organizationally means not to presuppose (an) organization as given
framework and outcome but to employ the notion of organization
as a preposition, which propels one to follow and trace the
processes of organizing and being organized.[4] As Latour puts it
somewhat contortedly, this implies trying "to follow a particular
being that would transport a force capable, in its displacements, of
leaving in its wake something of organization no matter what the
scale" (389–90). He suggests following the circulation of multiple
"scripts" of organizing, performative narratives that engage actors
and in whose "scripting" actors participate (Latour 2013a, 391). Yet
of course such scripts rely on material, technical, and embodied
practices and infrastructures; they are mediated, affective, and
discursive.[5] These modes or scripts shape, yet are never limited
to, formal entities such as corporations, state administrations, or
clubs. As Latour puts it, organizations "remain always immanent
to the instrumentarium that brings them into existence." Hence
organizations are "flat" (Latour 2013b, 49).

This epistemological angle might sound familiar to a media-theoretical perspective according to which a media-technological "instrumentarium" "determine[s] our situation" (Kittler 1999, xxxix). Yet it risks overlooking the recursive relation between media technology and social, or sociotechnical, ordering. As Reinhold Martin has shown with regard to the "military–industrial complex" in the U.S.-American context of the twentieth century, scripts or modes of organizing can constitute an "organizational complex" of power and knowledge. Such a complex both relies on and employs media technologies to shape what can be perceived and expressed. As "the aesthetic and technological extension of what has been known since the early 1960s as the 'military–industrial complex'" (Martin 2003, 3–4), this organizational nexus enables the emergence of specific—consumerist, individualized, self-organized—subject positions as well as new forms of networked, deregulated control (Deleuze 1995). In this sense, organization is as immanent to the "instrumentarium" as is its productive agent and driving force. Thinking and speaking organizationally thus means assembling Latour's "flat" and invariably mediated scripts and tracing, or speculating on, their convergence into a constellation of social organization. This, I think, is what Denny's work and, in particular, *Secret Power* negotiates and asks us to consider.

Products for (and of) Organizing

To prepare a closer look at *Secret Power* and its scripts of sociotechnical ordering, I briefly dwell on another Denny installation that directly poses the question of organization. In *Products for Organizing,* on display at London's Serpentine Gallery from the end of 2015 to early 2016, the exhibition space is (again) divided into two sections called *Products for Emergent Organisations* and *Products for Formalised Organisations.* Echoing *Secret Power*'s exhibition architecture, the former is made up of a series of vitrines designed for hard-drive stacks. The vitrines display a kind of sociomaterial history of hacking and hacker communities, yet one that is presented as an organizational history, which focuses on what Denny calls "organisational moments" (Gad 2015). It touches upon, for example, the Tech Model Railroad Club of the Massachusetts Institute of Technology, formed in the late 1940s and sometimes seen as the invention of hacking culture; the "blue box" sold on the University of California, Berkeley campus by Steve Wozniak and Steve Jobs as a way of getting free long-distance calls; early hacking groups who broke into the Los Alamos National Laboratory; the invention of computer bulletin board systems as organizational devices; and cryptography and the "cypherpunks" of the 1980s and 1990s.

Along pieces of hardware now packaged as commodities—Wozniak and Job's box here looks like a proper Apple product—there are documents that resemble technical manuals relating to key themes within the history of hacking. By "speaking organizationally" about such events, Denny not only insinuates that hacker groups developed their own "products for organizing"; he also seeks to trace and visualize the hacker movement's organizational logics, presenting their emergence as a "product of organizing," as it were. In this sense, "the objects that populate these narratives are presented as products capable of delivering certain organisational results: models for use, with packing suited to the reimagining" (Gad 2015, 190).

In the section on *Products for Formalised Organisations,* Denny assembles three case studies of proper organizations: Apple; Zappos, the shoe sales company owned by Amazon; and Government Communications Headquarters (GCHQ), the British intelligence and security organization, which also appears in *Secret Power.* The cases reproduce "flat" managerial and operational models apparently at work in these organizations and designed to work flexibly and nonhierarchically. A tool called Agile is an outgrowth of collaborative software-development methods, now translated into a kind of operating system for everyday organizational life. Another one, called Holacracy, endeavors to reconfigure an organization's work relations in an antihierarchical and self-organized way. No matter whether the organization typologically belongs to the public or private sector, whether it is a sales platform or a security agency, postdigital organization here seems ordered according to models of distributed authority. Moreover, the organizations' headquarters are on display in the form of architectural models, which perhaps not surprisingly take a loosely ring-shaped, circular form. This form is itself reproduced in internal visualizations, employed as a metaphor for the smooth and unhindered circulation of ideas.

In translating such "organizational moments" into visual, sculptural form—into "a monument to organisational life" (Gad 2015, 190)—Denny seems to embrace their materiality, images, metaphors, and human protagonists. The installation presents the interrelations of technology and organization as a pressing matter of concern in the age of pervasive and pervasively commercialized computing and therefore as self-evident subjects of contemporary artistic inquiry.

[Figure 2.2]. Simon Denny, *Products for Organising,* formalized org chart, architectural model—GCHQ 2/Agile, 2015. Photograph by Nick Ash.

The dichotomy of the two sections recalls Ned Rossiter's (2006) distinction of "organized networks" and "networked organizations." Organized networks employ the sociotechnical means of connectivity for new practices of organizing. They "are shaped by the power of socio-technical needs, interests, affects and passions that hold the potential to translate into new institutional forms" (208). Networked organizations, alternatively, "become networked in an attempt to recast [themselves] while retaining [their] basic infrastructure and work practices" (207). To some extent, Denny's exhibition reproduces this distinction. Contemporary media technologies, that is, provoke both new forms of organizing (here manifested by the emergent and antihierarchical scene of hacker culture) and the partial transformation of established corporations and state administrations. Yet in thinking organizationally, or so I would argue, the artist undermines the spatial juxtaposition between two sections that stand for apparently antithetical organizational setups. Is it (still) the case that it is organized networks (and not networked organizations) that are marked by an atmosphere of openness, practices of sharing and more loosely project-based activities (Lovink and Rossiter 2011)? "In cartoons, flowcharts and glass-cased models, all inscribed with jaunty narratives, he portrays what ought to be opposing movements—the top-down structure of big business and the free, flat world of hacking—showing where they meet in the middle in corporations such as Apple" (Cumming 2015). Arguably, this "middle" is constituted by media: by a set of shared technologies that enable *organizing* (note the exhibition title's gerund) in different contexts and thus afford techies, entrepreneurs, and bureaucrats to jointly usher in a new age of sociotechnical organization.

Of course, the juxtaposition of emergent and formalized organization can be read as a story of co-optation: of countercultural experiments and "moments" turned into instrumental tools to foster commerce, consumer captivation, and state surveillance. However, the genealogy of technology development in its cultural context tells a more complex story, according to which the legacy of the

military–industrial complex and that of the American counterculture comes together to spawn the "new economy" (Turner 2006).
Denny's installation seems closer to this kind of narrative. It draws
parallels between—indeed, presents a fluid milieu of—commercial
entities and hacker groups, bureaucrats and techies, and otherwise
refrains from any conventionally critical position or statement.
Of course, Denny could be accused of too easily believing in the
relentless self-mythologization of the corporate world and a
management discourse built on the rhetoric of participation and
collaboration, thereby masking or disavowing the everyday life of
hierarchy, domination, and control that shapes formal organizations. But precisely because there is no simple mechanism of cause
and effect between collaborative technologies and the leveling
of organizational hierarchies, *Products for Organizing*'s sculptural
rendering of the scripts that circulate in emergent and formal
organization hints at a broader organizational complex.

Secret Power's Scripts of Organizing

As *Products for Organizing* perhaps most clearly shows, thinking
organizationally can be described as "both . . . subject matter and
methodology of [Denny's] work" (*e-flux* 2015). Moving back to *Secret
Power,* my intent is not to comprehensively discuss the wealth of
connections, allusions, and the play of secrecy and transparency
that the show stages. Assuming an organizational perspective as
outlined above is itself an ordering device. It yields a specific lens
on how the exhibition thematizes organization, and how it is itself
organized. In this sense, the exhibition's objects and relations suggest three scripts of organization and media: secrecy, sensemaking,
and entrepreneurship.

Organizational Secrecy

The first script is connected to "the unlimited escalation of digital
surveillance" (Galison 2016, 156). This is one effect of what Galloway and Thacker (2007) have called the "new physics of organiza-

tion" based on flat and distributed network technologies. However, as Denny's installation insinuates, the new physics of organization can be closely intertwined with sovereign rule and bureaucratic control; networks have become a medium of sovereignty (Galloway and Thacker 2007, 20–21). In this sense, the exhibition pictures the way the globe is protocologically organized and policed through distributed networks. This logic of capture is at work both in state administrations and private corporations, which often actively cooperate, as Snowden revealed.

The server vitrines dedicated to material released by Snowden present an attempt to examine "the way the contemporary world is depicted in imagery used by the NSA" (Higgins 2015). They make visible a networked topology of control and intervention as imagined by the Five Eyes intelligence agencies. One focus is on Treasure Map, regarded as one of the more shocking of Snowden's revelations. This initiative is designed to map, monitor, and intercept no less than the global data traffic, "which seeks to create a comprehensive world map of connected devices, with many layers of data and metadata" (Barr and Denny 2015, 97). Apart from turning the skull motif of the internal Treasure Map presentation into a sculptural piece of the iconic T-800 skull from *Terminator 2,* Denny both reproduces explanatory slides leaked by Snowden and illustrates the program's operational logic through amplifying its infrastructural layers. Then there are exhibits from—and interpretations of—various, by-now infamous clandestine operations such as Fox Acid, Mystic and PoisonNut, designed to weaponize information technology. In assembling the Fox Acid material into a colorful and quite shocking mix of cartoons, crude jokes, explanatory tableaus, and infographics about network architectures, Denny emphasizes the operational setup for infiltrating personal computers through the back door of commercial internet providers (Kraus 2015, 23) in order to monitor and record all online activity, even to allow NSA operators to ghostwrite emails and social media postings "for" their victims, enabling a technologically advanced level of smear-campaigning.

[Figure 2.3]. Simon Denny, *Secret Power,* installation view, Marciana Library, 2015. Photograph by Jens Ziehe.

The script of organizational secrecy as presented by *Secret Power* inverts and turns on its head the popular discourse of "organizational transparency" enabled through digital media. Transparency here does not imply user knowledge of the system but rather user ignorance (Rouvroy 2011). Organizational transparency is not transparency "for" the public but transparency *of* citizens *for* state bureaucracies (and corporate players), which themselves operate clandestinely through means of protocological control and intervention. While a media history of organization could be written along different sociotechnical formations of secrecy and transparency (Beyes and Pias 2019)[6]—indeed, the function of pyramidal hierarchies might lie in determining and mediating formal points of exchange and a modicum of transparency, thereby cloaking the rest of organizational conduct in informality and secrecy—today's technological apparatuses enable and help to produce, in Peter Galison's words, "a form of secrecy with no end date, no limit of scope, and little access." Protocological organization is based on "a

new ontology of hidden knowledge: multiple infinite secrets for a
boundless conflict" (Galison 2010, 970). Arguably, it is this script of
organization that, as Geert Lovink (2016, "Hermes on the Hudson")
wrote after the NSA scandal had broken, has "dashed to pieces"
"the values of the internet generation," which were predicated on
"decentralization, peer-to-peer, rhizomes, networks."

Organizational Sensemaking

Yet *Secret Power* is not only about networks of secrecy and control
as imagined by the Five Eyes. Alongside the depictions of mass-
surveillance programs and the policing of the globe, the vitrines
entail a montage of objects and elements related to the intelligence
agencies' internal operations. Thus a second script of organization
and media manifests itself in the visual aesthetics of internal intelligence agency communication and the way these organizations
make sense of their operations. Foreshadowing the (later) *Products
for Organizing,* the focus here falls on a kind of management style:
how such state bureaucracies imagine and render visible their
tasks and processes. Steeped in geek-gamer tropes, internet
memes, historical fantasies, and military and animal imagery, the
way that cyberespionage operations are conveyed to the NSA's
employees and subcontractors is perhaps the viscerally most
shocking experience of Denny's handling and amplification of this
material. As the Treasure Map and the FoxAcid iconography, as
well as the maps, magicians, and soldiers that populate the slides
leaked by Snowden, indicate, the myths, memes, and fantasies of
the NSA itself come across as equally dark and brutal as they are
childish, playful, and colorful—and, of course, heavily remediated.
In Keller Easterling's (2015, 182) words,

> some of the most pervasive and under-examined aesthet-
> ic regimes successfully migrate across military and com-
> mercial environments as well as diametrically opposed
> political camps in ways that camouflage the real mes-
> sages or actions of organisations. In these tableaus, the
> accoutrements of history often look like the middle-aged

mottos, pyramids and mandalas of managementese, mixed with the sort of drawings that can be found under the bed of a teenage boy.

Yet as Byrt (2016) argues, the visual references are far from accidental: "They are targeted, precise and extraordinarily readable for the young men and women charged with implementing and overseeing such an epic surveillance system." It is remarkable, moreover, how these figures and objects are partly at odds with and partly correspond to the allegorical Renaissance paintings in the library, establishing a strange iconographic dialogue of bearded men and fantastic, cartoonish animals as guardians and icons of power/knowledge.

In this sense, the tone of *some* of the allegorical depictions and *all* of the Five Eyes material is "unashamedly self-congratulatory" (Bennewith and Metahaven 2015, 27) and drenched in a kind of relentless optimism. It should give orthodox management theory pause—but I am afraid it won't—that the management and leadership models deployed within the NSA and the British Government Communications Headquarters (GHCQ), as far as I can see, quite faithfully resemble what students of business and management are confronted with. Perhaps the agencies are at the forefront of a certain kind of instrumental organizational thought, too. A model presented in the GHCQ's The Art of Deception program, also leaked by Snowden and remediated by Denny, is constructed around the notion of "sensemaking." The sensemaking approach is a prominent way of theorizing how organization works and how processes of organizing discursively unfold. Yet The Art of Deception bluntly shows what the field of organization studies, it seems, only recently discovered (Holt and Cornelissen 2013), namely, that the making of sense is aesthetically predicated on what can be sensed. As a dark art, it is prone to affective and atmospheric modulation. Such managerial reasoning, in other words, seems well aware that forces of organization increasingly work on the level of what N. Katherine Hayles (2006) called the "technological nonconscious." Today's atmospheric and immersive media are key

agents of "a new affective organization" of the social (Angerer 2015,
115). Intelligence agencies, or at least the Five Eyes of the United
States, the United Kingdom, Australia, New Zealand, and Canada,
one can surmise from *Secret Power,* know and work with this kind
of knowledge to make sense of and enact networked conditions of
control and deception.

Entrepreneurs of Onflow

Apart from the invisible physics of organization and the internal
organizational sensemaking and its aesthetics, there is a third
script of organization and media at work in *Secret Power.* This script
seems closely related to Denny's prior work on the digital economy,
its processes, subjects, and hyperbolic claims. It pertains to the not
so secret star of the show, whom Denny and Bennewith discovered
in their research and subsequently turned into a centerpiece of
the installation: the designer David Darchicourt. Now running his
own firm based in Maryland, Darchicourt was a graphic designer
for the NSA from 1996 to 2001 and its creative director of defense
intelligence from 2001 to 2012, "creating original graphics for NSA
top leadership," according to his social media profile. The server
racks on the right-hand side of the library assemble work that he
has done for and within the agency, some pieces of his freelance
work, exhibition designs for the NSA Cryptologic Museum at its
headquarters in Fort Meade, and his LinkedIn profile. Furthermore,
Darchicourt was commissioned by Denny to create graphic rep-
resentations for what was labeled a New Zealand history project.
The designer responded in style. Based on an iconic New Zealand
reptile, he came up with a grinning cartoon lizard (or perhaps a
lizard-eagle) with a camera-shaped eye apparatus, looking for
prey—a kind of cyborg enhancement of the lizard.[7]

In the figure of Darchicourt, and through his design and his
products, the installation presents a both comical and disturbing
montage of the marriage of military gamer aesthetics, fantasy culture, disinformation, and libertarianism. It stages a meeting of surveillance and business that is conducted online, through platforms

[Figure 2.4]. Simon Denny, *Secret Power,* installation view, Marciana Library, 2015.
Photograph by Jens Ziehe.

such as Behance, Freelancer, and Mechanical Turk—platforms that
many (postdigital) artists use to commission material. Denny's ambivalent fascination with new media entrepreneurs here arguably
takes on a critical spin. Through the persona of the designer and
his works, the exhibition relates the dark operations and imageries
of state intelligence agencies to digital culture's demand to become

entrepreneurial selves. One of the board games on display is called Positive Press—Darchicourt is at home in different genres, if always with full-spectrum colors. The board game seeks to lead its young users from the "Down and Out Dump" to "Upbeat City," where "YOU report the news in a positive way!" In Kraus's words, "*Positive Press* is a lurid, disturbing game, simultaneously promoting the libertarian notion of 'wellness' and 'happiness' as *healthy personal choices,* and instructing primary school children in the rewards and production of 'spin-control' disinformation" (Kraus 2015, 24, emphasis original). Also on display: through Lifeskills Cardgames, today's Crypto-Kids, the "future codemakers and codebreakers," learn to "Dive into Social Networking" to become "Smart Sharks." As Nigel Thrift (2011, 16n29) has remarked, the effects of what he calls the "security–entertainment complex" are most visible in a media-savvy pedagogy that seeks to "prepare[] the child for a world in which they will need to be able to present publicly, seek out data, and produce new kinds of significance about what it means to be a subject. They need to be not so much learners of determinate knowledge as little entrepreneurs of onflow."

Organizing the Security–Entertainment Complex

If the kind of media-organizational nexus staged by *Secret Power* would need a speculative, generalized name, the one that comes to my mind is indeed the notion of the security–entertainment complex. It denotes, writes Thrift (2011, 11), "an era of permanent and pervasive war and permanent and pervasive entertainment, both sharing the linked values of paranoiac vigilance and the correct identification of the potential of each moment." The principle of persistent consumer and citizen surveillance in the name of security and consumption would constitute "the heart of an authoritarian capitalism" that has emerged over the last twenty or thirty years (Thrift 2011, 12). This perpetual surveillance is closely connected to what, with Grégoire Chamayou's (2015, 37–45) *Theory of the Drone,* can be called the principles of "data fusion" (merging different layers of data into one form of information); of "the schematisation of forms of life" (a kind of cartography of life through data patterns and "pattern recognition"; see Apprich et al. 2018); of creating a total "archive or film of everyone's life" (with the technologies of football broadcasting, or so Chamayou reports, seen as forerunner); and of "preemptive anticipation," according to which technology figures out what consumers want before they know they want it, or where potential perpetrators, whose data coalesce into the wrong patterns, are hunted down before any wrongdoing might or might not happen. In similar terms, Shoshana Zuboff (2015) has focused on Google to identify the outlines of what she calls *surveillance capitalism,* in which consumer anticipation is managed and modified by the predictive capacities of protocological control. This is what has turned Facebook "into the biggest surveillance-based enterprise in the history of mankind" (Lanchester 2017, 8).

Based on the ubiquity and availability of data as well as the means of information targeting and affective modulation, then, both security and entertainment sectors share the forms and outcomes of intelligence gathering, its research strategies and software codes. Agencies of state security and the behemoths of digital capitalism are the security–entertainment complex's main organizational players. Yet the kind of organizational forces at play here work on different levels. The security–entertainment complex fuses different organizational scripts into an organizational complex. Expanding on my reading of *Products for Organizing* and *Secret Power*'s organizational scripts, I distinguish between the three modes of protocological, bureaucratic, and entrepreneurial ordering.

First, the secret generation, mapping, and analysis of data is part of a new physics of organization. The corresponding property of organization and its forms of control and entrainment is software protocols. "Protocological organization" (Galloway 2011, 95) is "as real as pyramidal hierarchy, corporate bureaucracy, representative democracy, sovereign fiat, or any other principle of social and political control" (Galloway and Thacker 2007, 29). Protocological organization constitutes processes of organizing beyond and across the boundaries of organizational entities and below the threshold of human perception. The organized world is constructed here through distributed networks that continually and autonomously produce and relate data—put into the informational forms of observations, classifications, profiles, evaluations, and predictions—according to a set of parameters yet otherwise largely devoid of human interference. As Friedrich Kittler (2006, 49) wrote, it is now "media technologies constructed on the basis of formal languages" that "move the boundary between the possible and the impossible, the thinkable and the unthinkable." The corresponding regime of visibility and intelligibility, and the distribution of what can be perceived and expressed, takes the form of statistical or "algorithmic governance" (Rouvroy 2011). This is indeed a media a priori of contemporary sociotechnical ordering, and it is "so obvious that it seems to have drifted into the realm of the collective unconscious" (Lovink and Rossiter 2011, 280). While this modality of organizing might operate "flatly" and be spread out horizontally, to use Latour's terms, it is by no means a symmetrical script where nonhuman, automated algorithms would meet human bodies on equal footing, in a merry dance of agencies. Principles of targeting, permanent watch, schematization, and preemptive anticipation are coded into these organizational scripts. In the sphere of consumption, they help hold consumers "interidiotically stable" (Thrift 2008, 12). In the sphere of infotainment, "controlled by a handful of governments and corporations," they train citizens to become "village idiots" (Foster 2017, 75). In the world of labor, they seek to ensure docile employees and workers (Irani 2015). And employed in the militarized arms of the security–entertainment complex, they have deadly consequences (Chamayou 2015).

Second, this does not imply that conventional organizational entities and management styles disappear or necessarily lose influence. While there is some compelling evidence for the demise of the corporate form and the rise of platform-based, decentralized, and project-based organizational formations (Davis 2013), the performativity of automated algorithms has become central for bureaucratic rule, even a feature of bureaucraticization (Totaro and Ninno 2014). Such analyses bolster David Graeber's claim that far from reducing bureaucratic ordering, new information technologies and their logics of mapping, graphs, and codes help enact a kind of merger of public and private bureaucracies, ushering in an "era of total bureaucratization" (Graeber 2015, "Introduction"). Initiatives of so-called marketization or decentralization invariably lead to the expansion of bureaucratic ordering. Thinking organizationally, it is thus far from clear that practices of the social have now shifted away from formal organizational contexts and established institutions. Rather, the bureaucratic apparatuses of state security have adopted the technologies and imageries of networked organization to their own ends of surveillance and control. Just like social networking sites and platforms, they rely on apparatuses of capture that afford, to requote Thrift (2011, 11), the "linked values of paranoiac vigilance and the correct identification of the potential of each moment." And not unlike, for instance, Facebook,[8] the employment of such technologies can take on a particularly perverse spin in the case of the NSA and its allies. The bureaucratic potential of algorithmic control is married to a keen insight into such technologies' potential to enact and harness the deliberate modulation of affective states and the engineering of emotions. In this sense, bureaucratic forms like intelligence agencies have embraced the potential of new technologies without giving up on their modus operandi. They are turning into networked organizations so as to more pervasively perform "the multiple kinds of surveillance that populate everyday life" (Thrift 2011, 11).

Third, and following up on Graeber's thesis, such technological–bureaucratic ordering (of tasks, bodies, and affects) is entangled with, rather than opposed to, the rise of the entrepreneurial subject (Bröckling 2016). After all, if more and more technologically enabled work relations seem to resemble some forms or imaginaries of expressing one's creative self, then this kind of flexibilized labor in turn does not diminish but places a greater demand on bureaucratic overview and control (Beyes and Metelmann 2018;

Hall 2016). In *Secret Power,* the figure of Darchicourt and the crossover between militaristic and entertainment styles embody the role of organized networks as new agents of entertainment and entrainment in the security–entertainment complex. Based on the comparably horizontal practices of networked organizing, a kind of mobile and entrepreneurial network sociality has emerged (Wittel 2001). To some degree, relationships can be organized unconstrained from price mechanisms or "traditional hierarchical models of social and economic organization" (Benkler 2006, 8). In critical terms, though, "the new spirit of capitalism is found in brainwork, self-measurement and self-fashioning, perpetual critique and innovation, data creation and extraction" (Galloway 2014, 110). An entrepreneurialized subject or, as Denny's installation seems to suggest, an artist of commodification is called forth. To some degree untied of the boundaries of conventional formal organizations, he or she combines work and play and aspires to be both individualistic and sociable, autonomous and embedded, responsible and adaptive, perpetually happy, target-driven, and, perhaps, deceitful (Gill 2011).[9]

Adopting yet slightly displacing Keller Easterling's (2004) notion of "the new orgman," it is tempting to read such a figure as the latest instantiation or an update of the "organization man," William H. Whyte's (1956) proverbial and stereotypical figure embedded in, and dutifully loyal to, the postwar corporation. In *Secret Power,* the designer and former NSA creative director cuts a both scary and comical figure, cheerfully overidentifying with the libertarian and cruel world of the security–entertainment complex, just as Whyte's organization man presumably overidentified with the corporation. Yet in situating this figure as pivotal to the rise of the organizational complex that fed the military–industrial complex, indeed, as its cyborg, Reinhold Martin (2003) has shown how the organization man's combined conformism and individuality as well as modularity and flexibility already helped prepare the ground for unfettered commercialization and consumption. If the entrepreneurial cyborg of the security–entertainment complex presents an update, then this is not only because the "new orgman" trades in logistics, flogging styles of management and protocols for networking, as Easterling (2004) writes. In more general terms, the organization man's "powers have multiplied even if [or just because] his 'mind and soul' is no longer exclusively beholden to the demands of The Organization" (Lovink and Rossiter 2011, 280). The Orgmen are embedded in and tied to the life of networks (and their modes of bureaucratic and affective control); they are molded and modulated by contemporary media technologies. They have partly been made redundant by protocological organizing and automated governance, and they increasingly embrace a datafied, platform-based version of acting "as if they were all entrepreneurs" (Denny and Obrist 2016).

In this sense, the security–entertainment complex brings with it its own updated organizational nexus. This nexus shapes and is shaped by pervasive and ubiquitous digital technologies. It is geared toward permanent surveillance of citizens and consumers and its corollaries of preemptive anticipation and affective modulation. It cannot be reduced to either a logic of entrepreneurialism, or one of bureaucratization, or one of purely algorithmic control. Rather, the organizational nexus of the security–entertainment complex coalesces around modes of protocological, bureaucratic, and entrepreneurial orderings and their entanglements.

The Undemocratic Surround

As a way of pulling these strings together, I think that Denny's immersive installation can also be understood as an inversion of what Fred Turner (2013) has called the "democratic surround": the emergence of multimedia environments as forms of democratic communication in the United States. Developed during World War II by state agencies, intellectuals, and artists, the democratic surround was designed to support the molding of the "new man" as a democratic citizen who would weather the detrimental authoritarian effects of the mass media, as demonstrated in fascist

Germany. Supplementing the one-way, single-source channels of mass media with multimedia environments, or so it was hoped, would allow emancipated spectators to integrate a heterogeneous variety of sense perceptions into individual acts of sensemaking. Such immersive experience would resemble the political process of finding one's way in a diverse and complex society, and it would train the subject in partaking in it, even embracing it. Idea and practice of the democratic surround would later bleed into the counterculture and the multimedia utopianism of the 1960s and their experiments to expand human consciousness and foster a sense of belonging to human collectivity. In this sense, Turner (2013, 9) argues, "the democratic surround was not only a way of organizing images and sounds; it was a way of thinking about organizing society." As such, it not only represented a genuinely democratic impulse. It also came to be invested with what Turner calls a "managerial mode of a control: a mode in which people might be free to choose their experiences, but only from a menu written by experts" (6).

If this instrumental vision of expert control and leadership (of what the population should think and feel) has come to haunt contemporary sociotechnical life, as Turner suggests, then *Secret Power*'s postdigital assemblage presents an update of the relation between art, organization, and social transformation. Yet any democratic or emancipatory vision seems to have been purged. In today's organizational complex, the democratic surround has become a security–entertainment surround, and the new man a new org(wo)man. This surround is produced through different modalities of organization: scripts of invisible protocological organizing that are built to identify, classify, and sometimes taint or destroy human beings; networked organizations and organized networks as transformed or new forms of organization that increasingly rely on technical media as means of modulation and control; and a networked, horizontal mode of organizing entrepreneurial subjects, little entrepreneurs of onflow.

Can the Security–Entertainment Complex Be Represented?

The notion of surround also relates to the problem of how to research and represent today's invasive media and their partly invisible and partly preconscious—or nonconscious, to use Hayles's term—operations. How to render the organizational complex, if it is to some degree predicated on what seems beyond or before representation? How to write organization? On one hand, it seems a commonplace to point out that much of what was once regarded as the domain of social science, namely, generating and analyzing data, and thus an increasing part of the output of what was formerly carried out by social researchers—surveys, questionnaires, interviews, and so on—is now primarily in the hands of the security–entertainment complex, that is, agencies of state and, of course, Google, Facebook, and the like. In what amounts to a kind of perverse success story of scholarly inventions that have bypassed their inventors, we have arrived at a "new form of mediology in which the details of the everyday life of millions of people are . . . uploaded and analysed" (Thrift 2011, 10). Yet this kind of mediology is invisible to and unattainable for public scholarship. In a memorable turn of phrase, Galloway (2014, 127) has spoken of the subsequent emergence of "low-agency scholars," researchers unable to make numerically valid statements extracted from adequate measurement devices and data sets.

On the other hand, there is the question of representation itself. In a text titled "Are Some Things Unrepresentable?," Galloway (2011) has dwelled on Jacques Rancière's (2007) critique of the trope of unrepresentability in an earlier text of the same title. Because data have no visual form, Galloway argues, it is on the level of data's translation into information where visualization takes place. However, depictions of information networks would all look the same; they would adhere to a uniform set of aesthetic codes. There thus would not be a proper poetics of information networks able to render today's societies of control and its organizational forces.

I wonder, though, whether *Secret Power* does not offer a response to what low-agency scholars can do, and to representing contemporary social ordering. According to Anna Munster (2013), what in this text is called *protocological organization* works imminently or intensively beyond perception (through data fusion, data mining, and pattern recognition) and extensively through relations with other social and technical elements. The symbolic and representational level can therefore be seen as secondary, subordinated. In this sense, it is on this subordinate level where Denny's assemblage of hardware, images, objects, texts, and sculptural renderings cohere. These are thus works neither of media genealogy nor of media ecology (Kraus 2015, 20), nor are they experiments in "data undermining," to use Munster's (2013, "Data Undermining") term. Denny does not engage with, for instance, countermapping networks or writing "counterprotocological" code. As noted, he engages in a kind of anthropology of media culture that assembles, remediates, and reorganizes elements of orgware into the different context of art spaces. What appears is a mimesis of what is given to sensory perception in the form of *orgart*. And Denny becomes an artistic orgman, mimetically reproducing and amplifying issues of connectivity, networking protocols, and corresponding management styles. There thus is some ambivalence to Denny's work—perhaps a "strategic ambivalence" (Byrt 2016, "No Place to Hide") that itself becomes part of the artworks.[10] More than "just showing," Denny amplifies and reinterprets, connects and juxtaposes, the found material. It is thus a practice of "mimetic exacerbation" that can veer toward what Hal Foster (2017, 95), with a nod to the art of Jeff Koons, calls "an affirmation, even celebration, of the capitalist garbage bucket." Yet through its thematic, visual, and iconographic assembly, the work provokes reflections on the interrelations of what is on display—such as identifying different scripts of organizing. It is through gathering, alienating, and juxtaposing material into a different context, then, that different organizational scripts and their interrelations become manifest. It allows the visitor to think back, as it were, to the new physics of organization underneath of what is given to the human sensorium, to its operative setup as well as to its intimate relation with bureaucratic ordering, affective control, and entrepreneurial selves.

The "undemocratic surround" of *Secret Power* also invites consider-ations of the practice of ordering and of tracing connections itself. It performs an act of "reverse espionage" (Higgins 2015), of intelli-gence gathering and data fusion. Consider the speculative portrait of Darchicourt constructed through the designer's work, his traces online, and the leaked material as well as visually merging the designer's freelance material with the visual language employed by the intelligence agencies. As a visitor, then, one engages in one's very own, pedestrian, perhaps intelligence agency–like trawling through data and imagery, trying to connect dots and recognize patterns. It is a strangely seductive and uncanny exercise. Drifting through the exhibition, my experience was slowed down, rerouted, and opened to processes of association. This way, the imaginary, imagery, and styles of an organizational nexus that underpins the security–entertainment complex take on an evocative visibility and palpability.

Through an applied methodology of thinking organizationally, this kind of artistic research therefore posits a possible case of what the low-agency scholars, denuded of access to the data masses and the tools to analyze them, can do. Thrift (2011, 19) calls this the enactment of "cultural probes that can help people to rework the world by suggesting new unorientations rather than correctives"— a research labor of "suggestion, curiosity and wondering" (18). *Secret Power* posits organization as a preposition and urges the spectator to trace and connect scripts of organizing and being or-ganized. In the wake of these scripts, to paraphrase Latour (2013a, 390), something of organization is left, and it does not look pretty.

In Conclusion: Speaking Organizationally

This essay has dwelled on the question of thinking organizationally in the contemporary landscape of media-technological ordering. Intrigued by Simon Denny's installations *Products for Organizing* and *Secret Power* and their mimetic aggravations of orgware, I have discussed different modes of organization: protocological, bureaucratic, and entrepreneurial processes of ordering contemporary life. Yet these processes aren't mutually exclusive. They intermingle and cohere into a contemporary nexus of sociotechnical organization that can be understood as a manifestation and extension of the security–entertainment complex. For sure, there is no single logic governing the organizing of algorithms (Neyland 2015), just as there is no single mode of ordering in organizational settings. Consider for instance the financial markets and algorithmic or computerized high-frequency trading, the consequences of which might slip off the radar of the generalized notion of the security–entertainment complex. But then, tracing multiple scripts of organizing and the way they interrelate and might cohere is precisely what is required.

"Why do we still talk about organization in an era that seems to celebrate looseness and non-commitment?" Lovink and Rossiter (2011, 280) ask. Because the celebration of looseness and non-commitment does not equal the absence of organization but indicates the transformation of organizational scripts, perhaps the emergence of a new organizational complex. Lovink and Rossiter's focus falls on *orgnets,* organized networks and their potential to invent and establish new—emancipatory, progressive, transgressive—institutional forms. In similar terms, Rodrigo Nunes (2014) has outlined the notion of *network-movement* to think present-day organizing beyond formal organization—*The Organisation of the Organisationless* as not the absence of but a new mode of organization. After all, postdigital societies are not only a field of advanced techniques and strategies of manipulation, surveillance, and control. They still, one hopes, offer "plenty of opportunities for experimentation with political tactics and forms of organization" (Terranova 2004, 154).

However, it is not only net activism that "puts the Organization Question on the table" (Lovink 2016, "Occupy"). Another way of putting this is that networked forms of organizing are not the other to management and managerial domination, as Denny, tongue perhaps firmly placed in cheek, demonstrates so well. They might be cut from the same media-technological cloth. Indeed, "everyone is organizing" (Lovink and Rossiter 2011, 281). But then, there is a mirror and equally valid apodictic claim: everyone is being organized. The very same technologies that enable or perhaps condition new forms of relating and cooperating, indeed, the same scripts of ordering enabled or conditioned by such technologies, now constitute the heart and the intelligence of a security–entertainment complex in thrall to paranoiac watchfulness, to the surveillance, targeting, and affective control of consumers and citizens. In other words, contemporary organization is immanent to today's media-technological apparatuses just as much as it is their driving force. This is what is at stake when the term *organize* is mobilized in search of media, and why it is again time to think and speak organizationally.

Notes

1   In addition, *Secret Power* made use of a second venue: the arrivals lounge of Venice's Marco Polo Airport on the mainland, a contemporary space of transit and global security, where travelers are processed and monitored so as to enter EU territory. Here two photographic reproductions of the Library's ceiling and walls adorn the floor and the walls of the transit space. The juxtaposition of a "classic" site of power and knowledge with their contemporary manifestation is therefore inversed: a contemporary site of monitoring is invaded by depictions of Renaissance allegories. What might come across as a visual promotion for what's on in the Library (and hence for the artwork itself) takes on further meanings only in relation to the installation at the Biblioteca. After all, as Chris Kraus remarks, Marco Polo Airport was the world's first airport to employ digital surveillance and electronic access control (Kraus 2015), and Snowden stayed for forty days in the transit lounge of Moscow's Sheremetyevo International Airport (where he read Dostoyevsky's *Crime and Punishment,* or so it was reported; Luhn 2013).

2   Such works include *All You Need Is Data: The DLD Conference* (2012), a kind of twisted group portrait of movers and shakers of the digital economy; *The Personal Effects of Kim Dotcom* (2013), a re-creation and reimagination of the confiscated items of the notorious internet entrepreneur, which includes a collection of rather terrible works of art; *New Management* (2014), a study of Samsung manuals, training materials, and corporate reliquaries; *Disruptive Berlin* (2014),

sculptural portraits of ten young media companies; *Products for Organising,* an inquiry into the organizational logics that drive hacker communities and "proper" formalized organizations (see later); and *Real Mass Entrepreneurship* (2017), based on an investigation of small-firm technology production as mass phenomenon in Shenzen.

3   In this recursive sense, "media are not only the conditions of possibility for events—be they the transfer of a message, the emergence of a visual object, or the re-presentation of things past—but are in themselves events: assemblages or constellations of certain technologies, fields of knowledge, and social institutions" (Horn 2007a, 8).

4   Latour endorses a "process-theoretical" approach to the study of organization. This entails a shift from understanding organizations as bounded, stable entities (the corporation, the nonprofit organization, etc.) and their presumed properties to a focus on the "goings-on" of organizing. Such adverbial or gerundial thinking of organizing seems especially pertinent to changing organizational constellations that are enabled by and accompany media-technological transformations (Beyes 2017).

5   In this modified understanding, scripts resemble what fellow erstwhile ANT scholar John Law called "modes of ordering" (Law 1994). Latour's theatrical notion of scripts emphasizes a kind of Goffmanesque role-shifting, as organizational actors are sequentially scripting and being scripted in different capacities and engagements. This resembles a primarily temporal description of organizational role-playing, which now includes the capacity to work on the script itself. As such, the concept remains aspatial and atechnological (there seem to be no automated protocols in Latour's scripts). Law's notion of "modes of ordering" emphasizes the modes' or scripts' simultaneous multiplicity (and thus spatiality), their "strategic" effects (and thus power) as well as the technological configuration of these "material-semiotic" forces. It is in this sense that I first identify organizational scripts in Denny's work, before turning to contemporary modes of sociotechnical ordering.

6   As Georg Simmel pointed out, formal organization epitomizes the social form of the secret as "consciously willed concealment" (Simmel 1906, 449). In intelligence agencies, this willed concealment is doubled: a constitutive part of organizational life and the organizations' raison d'être (Horn 2007b). And with regard to bureaucratic power, Max Weber argued that it is in the "material nature" of every bureaucracy to keep its knowledge and intentions secret (Weber 1946, 233).

7   In a little scoop, a journalist from the *Guardian* contacted Darchicourt after she had interviewed Denny about the exhibition at the start of the Biennale: "While surprised, he was sanguine about the use of his work in the exhibition. 'I sell my work and I tend not to keep track of it,' he said. He added: 'I view myself as an Eskimo. They'd do their drawings on pieces of bone, and leave them in their campsites when they left. That's what I do. I was paid very well to do the work [for Venice] and David Bennewith was great to work with. As long as I have credit for my work I am happy'" (Higgins 2015).

8   In 2014, a study on "Experimental Evidence of Massive-Scale Emotional Contagion through Social Networks" caused a minor scandal. Coauthored by a Facebook researcher, the study discussed an experiment on nearly seven hundred thousand Facebook users (without their awareness) that entailed the purposeful manipulation of newsfeeds to find out if and how moods are transferred and travel across social networks (Kramer et al. 2014). Facebook, after all, is primarily in the advertising and surveillance business, which in a postdigital world relies on algorithmic practices of targeting, permanent watch, schematization, preemptive anticipation—and the modulation of moods.

9   In his reflections on *The Uberfication of the University,* Gary Hall quotes a futurologist who nicely (if probably inadvertently) captures the security–entertainment complex at work organizationally: "You might be driving Uber part of the day, renting out your spare bedroom a little bit, renting out space in your closet as storage for Amazon or housing the drones that does [*sic*] delivery for Amazon" (Hall 2016, 9).

10 "Consequently, I have never been able to entirely figure out whether he is a critic of the corporate neoliberalism that provides him with so much of his subject matter, or an artist deeply embedded with, and beholden to, that system" (Byrt 2016, "No Place to Hide"). As Byrt shows, departing from a clear-cut opposition between critique and affirmation might be a flawed or nonproductive way to engage with this kind of work. It seems to make more sense to ponder *Secret Power*'s "mimetic exercabation" (Foster 2017, 95) in terms of its potential as immanent critique of, in my reading, the security–entertainment complex.

References

Angerer, Marie-Luise. 2015. *Desire after Affect.* Translated by Nicholas Grindell. London: Rowman and Littlefield.

Apprich, Clemens, Wendy Hui Kyong Chun, Florian Cramer, and Hito Steyerl. 2018. *Pattern Discrimination.* Minneapolis: University of Minnesota Press/meson press.

Barr, Mary, and Simon Denny. 2015. "Mary Barr Talks to Simon Denny." In *Simon Denny: Secret Power,* edited by Robert Leonard and Simon Denny, 95–98. Milan, Italy: Mousse.

Benkler, Yochai. 2006. *The Wealth of Networks: How Social Production Transforms Markets and Freedom.* New Haven, Conn.: Yale University Press.

Bennewith, David, and Metahaven. 2015. "David Bennewith Talks to Metahaven." In *Simon Denny: Secret Power,* edited by Robert Leonard and Simon Denny, 27–33. Milan, Italy: Mousse.

Berry, David M., and Michael Dieter. 2015. "Thinking Postdigital Aesthetics: Art, Computation and Design." In *Postdigital Aesthetics: Art, Computation, and Design,* edited by David M. Berry and Michael Dieter, 1–11. Basingstoke, U.K.: Palgrave Macmillan.

Beyes, Timon. 2017. "'The Machine Could Swallow Everything': Satin Island and Performing Organization." In *Performing the Digital: Performativity and Performance*

Studies in Digital Cultures, edited by Martina Leeker, Imanuel Schipper, and Timon Beyes, 227–43. Bielefeld, Germany: transcript.

Beyes, Timon, and Jörg Metelmann, eds. 2018. *The Creativity Complex: A Companion to Contemporary Culture.* Bielefeld, Germany: transcript.

Beyes, Timon, and Claus Pias. 2019. "The Media Arcane." *Grey Room* 75, Spring 2019: 84–105.

Bröckling, Ulrich. 2016. *The Entrepreneurial Self: Fabricating a New Type of Subject.* Translated by Steven Black. London: Sage.

Byrt, Anthony. 2016. "No Place to Hide." In *This Model World: Travels to the Edge of Contemporary Art.* Auckland: Auckland University Press. http://www.press.auckland .ac.nz/en/browse-books/all-books/books-2016/this-model-world--travels-to-the -edge-of-contemporary-art.html.

Chamayou, Grégoire. 2015. *Drone Theory.* Translated by Janet Lloyd. London: Penguin.

Cumming, Laura. 2015. "Michael Craig-Martin; Simon Denny Review—Glowing Hot Meets Fastidiously Cool." *Observer,* November 29. https://www.theguardian.com/ artanddesign/2015/nov/29/michael-craig-martin-serpentine-simon-denny-review.

Davis, Gerald F. 2013. "After the Corporation." *Politics and Society* 41, no. 2: 283–308.

Deleuze, Gilles. 1995. "Postscript on Control Societies." In *Negotiations, 1972–1990,* translated by Martin Joughin, 177–82. New York: Columbia University Press.

Denny, Simon, and Hans Ulrich Obrist. 2016. "A Transcribed Conversation between Simon Denny and Hans Ulrich Obrist." *Cura* 21. http://curamagazine.com/ contents/a-transcribed-conversation-between-simon-denny-and-hans-ulrich -obrist/.

Easterling, Keller. 2004. "The New Orgman: Logistics as an Organising Principle of Contemporary Cities." In *The Cybercities Reader,* edited by Stephen Graham, 179–84. London: Routledge.

Easterling, Keller. 2015. "KOH-wa-ee." In *Simon Denny: Products for Organising,* edited by Amira Gad, 180–85. Cologne, Germany: Walther König.

e-flux. 2015. "Can Freedom Become a Burden? Simon Denny: Products for Organising." December 9. https://conversations.e-flux.com/t/can-freedom-become-a -burden-simon-denny-products-for-organising/2977.

Foster, Hal. 2017. *Bad New Days: Art, Criticism, Emergency.* London: Verso.

Gad, Amira. 2015. "Culturehacking: Inside (and Outside) Simon Denny's Work." In *Simon Denny: Products for Organising,* edited by Amira Gad, 186–94. Cologne, Germany: Walther König.

Galison, Peter. 2010. "Secrecy in Three Acts." *Social Research* 77, no. 3: 941–74.

Galison, Peter. 2016. "The Revelation of Secrets: Peter Galison and John May on Arti- facts of Surveillance, Part I and II." *Thresholds* 43: 136–59, 254–67.

Galloway, Alexander R. 2011. "Are Some Things Unrepresentable?" *Theory, Culture, and Society* 28, no. 7–8: 85–102.

Galloway, Alexander R. 2014. "The Cybernetic Hypothesis." *differences: A Journal of Feminist Cultural Studies* 25, no. 1: 107–31.

Galloway, Alexander R., and Eugene Thacker. 2007. *The Exploit: A Theory of Networks.* Minneapolis: University of Minnesota Press.

60   Gill, Rosalind. 2011. "Life Is a Pitch: Managing the Self in New Media Work." In *Managing Media Work,* edited by Mark Deuze, 249–62. London: Sage.

Graeber, David. 2015. *The Utopia of Rules: On Technology, Stupidity, and the Secret Joys of Bureaucracy.* Brooklyn, N.Y.: Melville House.

Hall, Gary. 2016. *The Uberfication of the University.* Minneapolis: University of Minnesota Press.

Hayles, N. Katherine. 2006. "Traumas of Code." *Critical Inquiry* 33, no. 1: 136–57.

Higgins, Charlotte. 2015. "Simon Denny, the Artist Who Did Reverse Espionage on the NSA." *Guardian,* May 5. https://www.theguardian.com/artanddesign/2015/may/05/edward-snowden-nsa-art-venice-biennale-reverse-espionage.

Holt, Robin, and Joep Cornelissen. 2013. "Sensemaking Revisited." *Management Learning* 45, no. 5: 525–39.

Horn, Eva. 2007a. "Editor's Introduction: 'There Are No Media.'" *Grey Room* 29: 6–13.

Horn, Eva. 2007b. *The Secret War: Treason, Espionage, and Modern Fiction.* Translated by Geoffrey Winthrop-Young. Evanston, Ill.: Northwestern University Press.

Irani, Lilly. 2015. "Difference and Dependence among Digital Workers: The Case of Amazon Mechanical Turk." *South Atlantic Quarterly* 114, no. 1: 225–34.

Kittler, Friedrich A. 1999. *Gramophone, Film, Typewriter.* Translated by Geoffrey Winthrop-Young and Michael Wutz. Stanford, Calif.: Stanford University Press.

Kittler, Friedrich A. 2006. "Thinking Colours and/or Machines." *Theory, Culture, and Society* 23, no. 7–8: 39–50.

Kramer, Adam D. I., Jamie E. Guillory, and Jeffrey T. Hancock. 2014. "Experimental Evidence of Massive-Scale Emotional Contagion through Social Networks." *Proceedings of the National Academy of Sciences of the United States of America* 111, no. 24: 8788–90.

Kraus, Chris. 2015. "Here Begins the Dark Sea." In *Simon Denny: Secret Power,* edited by Robert Leonard and Simon Denny, 19–25. Milan, Italy: Mousse.

Lanchester, John. 2017. "You Are the Product." *London Review of Books* 39, no. 16: 3–10.

Latour, Bruno. 2013a. *An Inquiry into Modes of Existence: An Anthropology of the Moderns.* Translated by Catherine Porter. Cambridge, Mass.: Harvard University Press.

Latour, Bruno. 2013b. "'What's the Story?' Organizing as a Mode of Existence." In *Organization and Organizing: Materiality, Agency, and Discourse,* edited by Daniel Robichaud and François Cooren, 37–51. London: Routledge.

Law, John. 1994. *Organizing Modernity.* Oxford: Blackwell.

Leonard, Robert. 2015. "Too Much Information." In *Simon Denny: Secret Power,* edited by Robert Leonard and Simon Denny, 11–16. Milan, Italy: Mousse.

Lovink, Geert. 2016. *Social Media Abyss: Critical Internet Cultures and the Force of Negation.* Cambridge: Polity Press.

Lovink, Geert, and Ned Rossiter. 2011. "Urgent Aphorisms: Notes on Organized Networks for the Connected Multitudes." In *Managing Media Work,* edited by Mark Deuze, 279–90. London: Sage.

Luhn, Alex. 2013. "Edward Snowden Passed Time in Airport Reading and Surfing Internet." *Guardian,* August 1. https://www.theguardian.com/world/2013/aug/01/edward-snowden-airport-reading.

Martin, Reinhold. 2003. *The Organizational Complex: Architecture, Media, and Corporate Space.* Cambridge, Mass.: MIT Press.

Munster, Anna. 2013. *An Aesthesia of Networks: Conjunctive Experience in Art and Technology.* Cambridge, Mass.: MIT Press.

Neyland, Daniel. 2015. "On Organizing Algorithms." *Theory, Culture, and Society* 32, no. 1: 119–32.

Nunes, Rodrigo. 2014. *The Organisation of the Organisationlessness: Collective Action after Networks.* London: Mute.

Rancière, Jacques. 2007. "Are Some Things Unrepresentable?" In *The Future of the Image,* translated by Gregory Elliott, 109–38. London: Verso.

Rossiter, Ned. 2006. *Organized Networks: Media Theory, Creative Labour, New Institutions.* Rotterdam: NAi.

Rouvroy, Antoinette. 2011. "Governmentality in an Age of Autonomic Computing: Technology, Virtuality, and Utopia." In *Law, Human Agency, and Autonomic Computing,* edited by Mireille Hildebrandt and Antoinette Rouvroy, 119–40. London: Routledge.

Simmel, Georg. 1906. "The Sociology of Secrecy and of Secret Societies." *American Journal of Sociology* 11, no. 4: 441–98.

Terranova, Tiziana. 2004. *Network Cultures: Politics for the Information Age.* London: Pluto Press.

Thrift, Nigel. 2008. "The Material Practices of Glamour." *Journal of Cultural Economy* 1, no. 1: 9–23.

Thrift, Nigel. 2011. "Lifeworld Inc—and What to Do about It." *Environment and Planning D: Society and Space* 29, no. 1: 5–26.

Totaro, Paolo, and Domenico Ninno. 2014. "The Concept of Algorithm as an Interpretative Key of Modern Rationality." *Theory, Culture, and Society* 31, no. 4: 29–49.

Turner, Fred. 2006. *From Counterculture to Cyberculture: Stewart Brand, the Whole Earth Network, and the Rise of Digital Utopianism.* Chicago: University of Chicago Press.

Turner, Fred. 2013. *The Democratic Surround: Multimedia and American Liberalism from World War II to the Psychedelic Sixties.* Chicago: University of Chicago Press.

Weber, Max. 1946. *Essays in Sociology.* Translated by H. H. Gerth and C. Wright Mills. New York: Oxford University Press.

Whyte, William H., Jr. 1956. *The Organization Man.* New York: Simon and Schuster.

Wittel, Andreas. 2001. "Toward a Network Sociality." *Theory, Culture, and Society* 18, no. 6: 51–76.

Zuboff, Shoshana. 2015. "Big Other: Surveillance Capitalism and the Prospects of an Information Civilization." *Journal of Information Technology* 30, no. 1: 75–89.

3

Organization Is the Message: Gray Media

Lisa Conrad

Epistemic Things

The concepts of *media* and *organization* are quite diffuse. This should not however be seen as a lack. Rather, they resemble "epistemic things" (Rheinberger 1997, 28). Situated between phenomenon and concept, they are what one does not yet know. Their irreducible vagueness carries the activity of research forward. So, what would happen if one would relate media and organization? More diffuseness and complexity, for sure. Yet, three distinct fields of inquiry or ways of seeing take shape. First, there is an organizational definition of media: they are the things that organize. This idea is mostly news to organization studies but not to media studies. The organizational understanding of media has been around for a long time; it has even helped shape the discipline's identity. Second, the question arises of how media are organized. How do institutions, conventions, power structures, and broader technological environments shape "the things that organize"? Here media are not understood as cohesive and self-contained but rather as entangled with their concrete settings of use and application—with their habitats. Third, a normative question appears that scrutinizes what it means for media to be *well* organized. In search of media and in terms of media, what is a *good organization*? While perhaps an unanswerable question, it raises the unavoidable issue of the "task of governance" (Rossiter 2006, 17).

To unpack these three approaches, and what they allow us to see, implies drawing on the fields of media studies, organization studies, science and technology studies, information systems research, and business history. Complementing and materializing this discussion, perhaps like an empirical test-bed of some of the claims extracted from the literature, I will weave in descriptions of, and reflections on, the phenomenon of enterprise resource planning software (ERP). Considering media in the context of formal (or traditional) organizations leads more or less inevitably to enterprise software. Over the past thirty years, these software packages have emerged as the new standard infrastructure of organization and administration. They are a paradigmatic example of gray media, a term Mathew Fuller and Andrew Goffey (2012, 1) use for those unremarkable media "most recognizable from the world of work and administration," such as databases, accounting records, forms, and planning tools. Today ERP and related software packages are crucial media of organizing, and we are in the middle of witnessing the reconfigurations that this will bring about.

Things That Organize

LISA CONRAD: I always find it awful to get acquainted with a new computer program. . . . It takes time. . . .

MRS. J.: I also dreaded Infor [enterprise software] back then. . . . Something new again, oh dear . . . but actually, it was easier than I had imagined. This is also what I'm thinking now [with the upcoming introduction of SAP]. Why shouldn't it work? . . .

LC.: Sure. And there are also some kinds of parallel systems, so it does not all depend on SAP. If SAP sort of—

J: Drops out?

LC: Yes, then you can still—

J: Then I can still—well I wouldn't be able to do any production orders. I could . . . without the system I couldn't
do anything. No, I couldn't do an order, because without
Infor or without SAP it isn't working. . . . I don't know. Well,
you cannot imagine the world without system anymore.
It doesn't work. No. Back to the work folder, that doesn't
work.

This conversation[1] between J. and me quite literally deals with
the technological condition of organizing. We are encountering
media theory's central thesis not between dusty book covers but
in the real world and in action. Without the system, you "couldn't
do anything." Going back to work folders is hard to imagine. The
processes of organizing are entirely enmeshed with networked
computers running on a common database, with workstations on
every desk displaying an interface for data entry and with every
newly entered piece of data turning into the informational base
of all the other workstations in real time. It is not conceivable, but
also not feasible, to work beyond this infrastructure. The account
should not be taken as an isolated, peculiar case. Extending from
their base in manufacturing, ERP systems have been adopted in
almost every productive and service sector (Pollock and Williams
2009). Today it would be difficult to find a company with more
than twenty employees that does not utilize some kind of business
software to manage stock, staff, customers, orders, processes, and
finance. The public sector, too, is widely equipped with software
packages stemming from private providers (Pollock and Williams
2009, 3). ERP systems are on the brink of turning into "mature
technological systems"—ordinary, unremarkable, and unlikely to
prompt wonder or inquiry (Edwards 2003, 185). They have become
everyday infrastructures.

Formal (or traditional) organizations and digital technologies are
thus thoroughly interlaced (e.g., Zuboff 1988; Orlikowski and Scott
2008; Conrad 2017). Mrs. J. says, "Without the system I couldn't
do anything. No, I couldn't do an order, because without Infor or

without SAP it isn't working." This kind of dependence is, of course, not new. Previous forms of organization emerged from and depended on paper (e.g., Kafka 2012; Hull 2012; Vismann 2008; Siegert 2006). Now networked computers equipped with enterprise-wide software are the central and standard means of organizing. "Back to the work folder, that doesn't work." There are numerous providers of these software packages, the biggest of which are Oracle, Microsoft, Infor, and SAP. However, SAP (Systems, Applications, Products in Data Processing) is widely recognized as dominating the market. Founded by five former IBM engineers from Mannheim, Germany, in 1972, SAP has become the new *sap* of organizational life, its vital force. SAP's most successful software products, R/2 and R/3, have defined what ERP software is and should do. The SAP chroniclers Ludwig Siegele and Joachim Zepelin (2009, 33) argue that SAP's software packages—creating new structures of organizational perception and action—have shaped the recent phase of economic and logistical globalization. The authors propose an analogy to double-entry bookkeeping: it has never been merely a tool of *documenting* what goes on in an organization, but it profoundly *transformed* businesses as well as the economy as a whole (cf. Quattrone and Puyou, forthcoming). In the same way, ERP systems have significantly *intervened* into the way global businesses run and interact with each other (Siegele and Zepelin 2009, 29).[2] "The best-run businesses run SAP," as one of the company's advertising campaigns has claimed.

How is the field of organization studies responding to this profound infrastructural shift in the setup of organizing? There is a dispersed stream of research that is interested in the "stuff" of organization. It looks at the intertwining of organizational practices and the technological infrastructures businesses rely on. In a short text on "Organizing as a Mode of Existence," Bruno Latour condenses many of these arguments that have been made in the tradition of ethnomethodology, practice theory, pragmatism, and process philosophy. The text acknowledges the "mass of work" that has been done in organization studies to complicate and rede-

scribe notions of organization (Latour 2013, 47).[3] One of the crucial
points that Latour carves out is the idea to conceive of organizations as "always *immanent* to the instrumentarium that brings them
into existence" (49, emphasis original). "There is no inertia at all
in an organization. But if you stop carrying it along: it drops dead"
(41). Accordingly, carrying out an organization means translating
it, hence taking it from one moment to the next. It is this focus on
the "tiny transcendence" (50) that leads to "the precise *tools* that
allow the organization to shift from one sequence . . . to the next"
(47, emphasis original). He lists writing devices, organizational
speech acts, instruments of accounting, and auditing as examples
for "those humble tools" on which organizational work relies (48).[4]
Thus Latour points to an emerging definition of organizing ensuing
from its means. Starting from concrete and "tiny" practices of organizing, this understanding conceives of organizational practices
as being inseparable from their material and technological means.
They are not independent of their instruments, of their carrier
media, neither today nor in the past. What we are able to do and
what we can imagine doing is "*immanent*" to the characteristics of
the tools at hand.[5]

To media studies, this line of argumentation is nothing new. The
intimate connection between technological infrastructures and
organization is a focal point of media studies. In fact, organization
would be a quite suitable term to define media studies' central
and identificatory concept, as John Durham Peters (2015) has
recently demonstrated. His book *The Marvelous Clouds* starts with
an elaboration of the "intellectual landscape" leading to the media
concept that is crucial to the book's argument and that reaches
"beyond messages to habitats" (14–15). Further outlining this
"expanded sense of the media concept," he describes media as
"vessels and environments, containers of possibility that anchor
our existence and make what we are doing possible" (1–2). With
recourse to Elihu Katz, Peters chooses "organization" to elaborate
on this. According to Katz (1987, 30), there are three paradigms
within media and communications research, namely, information,

ideology, and organization. Information is concerned with media as means of "transmitting information in a political system" (27). Ideology, alternatively, deals with the hegemony of certain media outlets as well as with practices of resistance to them. Last but not least, organization occupies "the more elementary idea that the essential attributes that characterize a predominant medium might affect social order, or, in other words, that the media may tell us both how to think and how to organize" (29). In this paradigm, the effects of media are considered to be "on organization—empire, market, science, church" (30).

For Peters (2015, 17), "Katz's diagnosis helps to show the edge space in which this book sits, namely, the third or technological tradition." This realm, Peters continues, has been developed by a range of different scholars, such as Lewis Mumford, James Carey, Harold Innis, Marshall McLuhan, André Leroi-Gourhan, Friedrich Kittler, and Bruno Latour (18). Even though "not all of [them] recognize 'media' as their central theme," they nevertheless have contributed to an understanding of media as "civilizational ordering devices" (5), "fundamental constituents of organization" (19), or "materials to manage time, space and power" (20). To these researchers, organization is the main effect of media. But maybe it makes sense to put it the other way around and claim that it is these scholars' interest in matters of organization that has led them to media. This would then point to an organizational definition of media. It is the capacity to order, to manage, to arrange, to structure, and so on, that turns an object into a medium.

The work of Harold Innis and its strong ties to the social and economic sciences encapsulates such an organizational definition of media. Indeed, throughout his career, Innis remained "faithful to his political economy origin" (Drache 1995, xiv). From the 1920s on, Innis was employed at the University of Toronto, where he later met and collaborated with Marshall McLuhan. He studied the history of the Canadian Pacific Railway (Innis 1923), fur trade (Innis 1930), and cod fishery (Innis 1940) in Canada.[6] In the course of this, he developed an explanation of the economic development of Canada that links it to its staples and basic goods, which are, in their turn, linked to the character of the landscape. For instance, "extensive waterways and the dominant Pre-Cambrian formation" provide the conditions for collecting furs in the northern regions and transporting them to the centers of trade (Innis 1950, 3; Innis 1930). He concludes that the character of the landscape, dominant staples, transportation systems, and means of communication crucially shape the specific development of states and societies. As if to test this argument, Innis then begins to devote himself to historic empires—especially their rise and fall—and how they relate to transformations in the material and technological environments. *Empire and Communications* (Innis 1950) traces stone, clay, parchment, papyrus, the alphabet, and paper in ancient Egypt, Babylonia, Mesopotamia, and medieval Europe but also the emergence of mass media from the fifteenth century on, such as printed books, newspapers, and, eventually, radio.

Innis's work is often received as consisting of two phases. The first phase is associated with his exploration of Canadian economic history and the development of the so-called staples approach. The second phase, starting with *Empire and Communications,* is considered as providing contributions to the theory of media and communication. But "to think that the later Innis was concerned strictly with cultural issues while the early Innis of the staples was narrowly focused on economic development is plainly wrong," stresses Daniel Drache (1995, xl), who revived and reframed the reception of Innis's work in the 1990s. Quite the contrary, it can be argued that throughout his career, Innis was interested in questions of organization. This is what unites his objects of research: waterways, natural resources, basic goods, trading routes, means of transport, means of communication, and practices of administration—they organize commercial and labor relations, social and political institutions, and cultural conventions. Each is an "organizing mechanism" (Drache 1995, xlv) generating different configurations of resources, people, knowledge, and power. Hence Innis is concerned with the connection between the way certain regions, cities, states, or empires are organized and the material features of those things that afford transport, exchange, overview, coordination, control, and so on. For "those things" he uses the term *media.* Therefore, to Innis, media are not only that which organize the mass democracies and consumer societies of the twentieth century but also that which organize early civilizations, antique city-states, medieval Christianity, the Industrial Revolution, or the Canadian economy. This means that an organizational definition of media includes "classic" mass media (e.g., newspaper, radio), gray media used in administration and business (e.g., stone tablets, papyrus, paper), and elemental media (e.g., rivers, mountains, valleys) alike (Peters 2015).[7]

In the reception of the Toronto School of Communication, Innis has taken on the role of Marshall McLuhan's boring older brother. However, the basic anchors of McLuhan's media theory "had already been developed, as McLuhan admitted, in the writings . . . of Innis" (Pooley 2016). These are the focus on carrier media instead of messages, the concentration on "the character of the material, particularly its relative permanence" (Innis 1950, 6), but also the vanishing point of *social organization,* a term both scholars use. For McLuhan ([1964] 1994, 8), the criterion to consider an artifact as a medium is the "change of scale or pace or pattern that it introduces." With *The Gutenberg Galaxy,* he explicitly undertakes "a study of the divergent nature of oral and written social organi-zation" (McLuhan [1962] 2002, 1). He claims that new dominant media cause a reconfiguration of perception and cognition. Via this twist of "the kaleidoscope of the entire sensorium" (55), media have significant effects on the organization of social life. For instance, before writing, there is an "intense stress on auditory organiza-tion of all experience" (24). Nonliterate societies—he describes them as gossipy, entranced, and obsessed with magic—are "the product of speech, drum and ear technologies" (8). Writing and printing, conversely, bring about a sociality that is structured by centralism, individualism, commercial spirit, and powerful scientific institutions. Eventually, Friedrich Kittler (1999)—working "in strict accordance with McLuhan" (xl–xli)—famously claims that "[media] determine our situation" (xxxix). In Kittler's writings, the primal interest in media as effectors of organization is carried on. Focusing on technical media in relation to cultural production, such as literature and music, he follows the poststructuralist program of questioning knowledge and truth.

McLuhan ([1964] 1994, 7) coined the slogan "the medium is the message." The cybernetician Norbert Wiener ([1950] 1989), on the other hand, titled one of his chapters "Organization as the Message."[8] Looking at these statements from the perspective of the organizational stream of media studies, they seem to be saying the same thing. It could be paraphrased as "the medium is organization and organization is the message." Research on cybernetics serves as a fruitful example to show where the organizational stream of media studies has been heading in the recent decades (e.g., Pias 2003; Hagner and Hörl 2008; Peters 2016). Cybernetics can be described as a 1950s-universalist scientific project but also as a powerful utopian narrative that inspired the application of its ideas in various fields of practice (Medina 2011; Kline 2015). Though the definitions are manifold, cybernetics developed a model of thinking (and designing) that revolves around the principle that machines/organisms/humans receive information from the environment, which then effects a regulation of behavior so as to adapt to the environment. These information-feedback loops are assumed to be at work in all kinds of systems—physical, biological, technological, and social. Hence the universalist claims of cybernetics. It carries the promise of explaining, but potentially also regulating and controlling, the behaviors of these systems.

Ronald Kline (2015, 6) considers cybernetic thinking as coevolving with the development of the first digital computers during that period of time. He relates the "cybernetic craze" of the 1950s—the unexpected popularity of its models and terms—to "a lively public discourse about the changing relationship between humans and machines, a discourse stimulated by the invention of electronic computers" (69). There was an enthusiasm about "some fantastic world of the future peopled by robots and electronic brains" (Boulanger, cited in Kline 2015, 7), but there were also worries about a sweeping automation that would lead to "devaluing brains in industry," as a newspaper headline has put it (Kline 2015, 71). Thus cybernetics—the science, the applications, and the fantasies—are part of an atmosphere of coming to grips with a new generation of machines "creating a new economic and social order" (5). By now, sixty years later, it has become common sense that ubiquitous networked computing technologies are triggering new value-creation chains, new business models, new divisions of labor, new forms of exploitation, new forms of governance, of activism, of criminality, and so on—in short, a new organization of life. Perhaps it is accurate to speak of a "process of cybernetization of all modes of existence" (Hörl 2016, 26). More and more areas of life are permeated and reorganized through networked computer systems. Wherever possible, computer-based information-feedback systems are applied to regulate flows of supply and demand by aggregating data, signaling capacities or constraints, and prompting appropriate reactions.

Thus the organizational stream of media studies that developed and established a concept of media as being fundamentally related to issues of organization has been around for a long time. In this sense, we could even consider the genealogy of media thinking as shaped by organization. Media scholars continue to scrutinize the things that organize. Exploring the way media create certain patterns of organization and how the lens of organization defines what we consider to be a medium is the first line of inquiry exposed by the relation between media and organization. It is a defining and strongly resonating feature of media research.

Media Are Organized

The second field of inquiry that the relation of media and organization carries with it complicates the first one. Media organize, but they are, in turn, also organized. This field draws on an under-

standing of media not as cohesive and self-contained effectors of
certain forms of organization but rather as messily interlaced with
social institutions as well as all sorts of other media. It can be found
within the aforementioned organizational stream of media studies
(e.g., Vogl 2007), but especially in more recent social science (and
STS) inflected research projects (e.g., de Laet and Mol 2000). Thus
the focus does not lie on causal effects but rather on "assemblages
or constellations of certain technologies, fields of knowledge, and
social institutions" (Horn 2007, 8). These constellations are always
on the move, so to say, with every part constantly shaping and
being shaped by all the others. By now there is, for instance, a real
substream of research looking at the way literary genres, concepts
of authorship, and the copyrights form and are formed by paper,
handwriting, or word processing software (e.g., Siegert 1999; Dommann 2014; Gitelman 2014; Tenen 2017). Interestingly, also Harold
Innis, whom I presented as standing for the position stressing the
organizational capacities of media, can be cited as being aware
of media's organizedness through social institutions. His staples
approach comprises the idea that a geographic and economic area
is rarely untouched by some prior "social framework that organized
land, labour, and capital" (Drache 1995, xix). There are old elites,
social conventions, and different cultural backgrounds interacting
with the less social structures, such as the character of the land
and its principal trading commodities. To carve out this less linear
and less causal understanding of media's relation to organization, I
will first come back to the case of business software—the example
this text has started out with. I will then move on to the work of
other scholars who have sketched and stressed the organizedness
of media.

Already when taking a very broad historical perspective on the
integration of computing technologies into the world of business,
a *mutual molding* and a *mutual organizing* become evident. Ever
since tinkerers and inventors came up with electromechanical computing technologies toward the end of the nineteenth century—
such as Herman Hollerith with the punched-card tabulator—these

technologies were envisioned as "business machines."[9] They were made in a way to swiftly enter the field of private and public organizations (e.g., Yates 2000; Heide 2009). Historians of business and technology have shown how information technology providers and user industries interacted with and pressured each other. On one hand, companies synchronized their processes as well as their products or services to the technological capacities available. On the other hand, research and development efforts of the technology companies were oriented toward application in corporate contexts. For instance, Yates gives an account of U.S. insurance companies being among the first organizations to integrate punched-card technology (from about 1910 onward). By the 1950s, the insurances' actuarial calculating practices as well as many of their business practices, such as billing, run on punched-card systems (Yates 1993, 49). Concomitantly, the need of this "'information-based' industry" to handle large amounts of data continued to rise (Campbell-Kelly 1992, 118). Therefore insurance companies were also among the first to purchase the newly available computers for civil use, Remington Rand's Univac (1951) and the IBM 650 (1953). Technologically, the IBM 650 was less sophisticated than the Univac, but it was compatible with the punched-card environment that had proliferated within these companies. It presented an "easy migration path" from punched cards toward the upcoming computer technologies (Yates 1999, 7). It created significantly more demand than the Univac, and by 1955, IBM had already taken the lead in computer sales (Yates 1999, 18). Thus, throughout the twentieth century, computer technologies have permeated offices, factories, and workshops. While they persistently widened their area of application—changing organizational practices one by one, creating new visibilities and possibilities for action—developments in computing were geared toward compatibility with the existing technological and organizational infrastructure.

Afore I had mentioned that SAP has set and become the standard of ERP software. But as research on standards has shown, there

is always some kind of "legacy system" that a new standard has
to lock into (Star and Lampland 2009, 16). It has to be backward
compatible with prevailing standards—be they technical or
institutional standards. In the case of SAP, the story goes like this:
the company's first customer, a fiber plant of Imperial Chemical
Industries (ICI) located in Östringen, Germany, had commissioned
a "Material Information and Accounting System." However, the
SAP founders and computer scientists Dietmar Hopp and Hasso
Plattner knew next to nothing about material management and
accounting. They needed to tap into this existing field of practice.
To do so, they first managed to hire the economist Claus Wellen-
reuther, also a former IBM colleague, holding a degree in business
administration. In this early stage of the company, his expertise on
the standards of business administration was indispensable. Hopp
says in retrospect that he would not have started the enterprise
without him (Siegele and Zepelin 2009, 47). Second, to comprehend
the existing standards of business that the new software would
have to take up, they undertook something akin to an ethnographic
exploration of its first customer. "They started in the middle of
the daily practice. Day after day the young entrepreneurs of SAP
talked with ICI employees in order to understand how the fiber
plant was pulsing and ticking and what it held together" (52). They
studied the very concrete procedures of business administration
and accounting in great detail. These insights were then translated
into the slowly evolving software package. Thus the SAP standard
software incorporated preceding practices of doing business,
such as established procedures, classifications, and norms. It did
not start from zero but inserted itself into an existing structure
by making sure that it was compatible with it (Star and Bowker
2002; Pollock, Williams, and D'Adderio 2007). Today SAP is said
to be "tightly anchored in the Old Economy"—in the structures of
the nineteenth- and twentieth-century corporations (Siegele and
Zepelin 2009, 90).

But the SAP standard software not only incorporates existing ways
of doing business; it also incorporates the existing geopolitical

order of the nation-state and—more importantly—of overcoming it through supranational governance. This aspect of being postnational is said to have been SAP's main advantage over other ERP software packages in the 1980s, and it is said to relate to its European origin. This simply means that the software was built in an environment where operating across national borders was promoted and facilitated by supranational regulation. Early on, SAP developed different country-specific versions (Mormann 2016, 81). Thus the software was made to display and to switch between different languages, currencies, measuring units, and county-specific fiscal and legal norms (70). In an interview in 1997, Plattner explains that SAP allows to handle different currencies, and moreover, it allows to deal with two currencies in one country: the new common currency, the euro, will run "on top, in parallel." Supposedly, this is "a complexity the American software doesn't handle well" (Plattner, cited in Mormann 2016, 72). SAP's continuous dissemination in the world of big business seems to be crucially related to its compatibility with transactions across nation-states. The software does not clash with national particularities such as language, currency, metrics, and legal norms. Quite the opposite, it serves as an adaptor between these national standards.

ERP software and especially SAP's market-dominating products R/2 and R/3 have profoundly reconfigured the way global businesses run. Nonetheless, as this section has aimed to show, ERP software itself is organized by various long-standing institutions, practices, conventions, rules, and so on. It has been construed in a way to fit the well-trodden paths of business and administration. It is socially, practically, and materially backward compatible.

Today press and politics do not talk about cybernetics anymore. Instead, the magic word is digitization. It marks the contemporary sentiment of living in a new period of techno-organization—the impression of experiencing a profound change in the way sociality is organized. Media scholars Geert Lovink and Ned Rossiter are among the first to take seriously the reorganization of sociality through so-called new media since the 2000s. They start from

the basic media-theoretical position that these media are hav- ing profound effects on the way we live and work. "Organized
Networks"—the term Rossiter (2006, 23) chooses to describe a
new technological and social mode of organizing—"institute new
modes of networked sociality." "That much is obvious," he resumes
(43), but what is neglected is the way previous institutional forms,
such as the nation-state or the business firm, continue "to play a
substantive role" (43). He considers digital media technologies as
situated within specific geopolitical, social, and economic contexts.
Their technical standards are "shaped by economic and political
interests," and patterns of stratification are preserved through an
"uneven geography of information flows" (35–36). Digital media
technologies are entangled with institutions such as property
rights, the (supra-)national provision of infrastructure, or "alpha
males scheming in the back rooms" (36). Hence digital networks
do not unfold on a blank page but rather enter and emerge from
a field populated with structures, institutions, conventions, and patterns of behavior. Media organize, that much is obvious, but they,
in turn, are organized by certain social structures. In a similar vein,
Geert Lovink (2012, 1) claims that "business interests from both the
Old and New Economy, in close harmony with governments and
the 'moral majority' will do whatever they can to limit the potentials
of new media." Thus, according to Lovink, the organizing potential
of new media is impaired by existing accumulations of power and
agency and the interest to preserve them.

Hence media organize. But media are not universal, uniform, or
given (Orlikowski and Iacono 2001, 131). They emerge from other
media and their respective institutions. In a way, they are inter-
locked with and held back by preceding media, institutions, and
their practices. Media are not just effectors of organization—of
a certain mode of perceiving, interacting, attributing, processing,
and so on—but media are inserted within a context that organizes
them. This context is made up of powerful structures and the
struggles over them; of institutions established decades and centuries ago; and of lifestyles, stocks of knowledge, habitus, and

forms of subjectivation corresponding to these institutions. Media are organized by the patterns and features of the places they are emerging from (Larkin 2004). These features and patterns are, for instance, subterrestrial power transmission grids, an administration running on punched cards, or a national currency. Media organize, but media are not of a piece, whole and monolithic. They are intermeshed with the context from which they emerge and in which they exist.

The Good Organization

Eventually, there is a normative aspect to the relation between media and organization, even if (or just because) this kind of normativity is often sidelined in media theory, or itself seen as entangled with mediatic conditions. Media organize and media are organized, but what does it mean for them to be *well* organized? What would constitute a "good organization"?[10] And how is this idea of the good organization (of the internet, or a company, or a community) influenced by the existing constellation of technologies and institutions? In the following section, I sketch some of the ways this notion has been and could be pursued.

To approach the thorny issue of what is good or desirable, the early thinkers of organizational media studies, Harold Innis and Marshall McLuhan, can be consulted once again. With regard to the development of the Canadian economy, Innis (1950, 3) says, "Each staple in its turn left its stamp, and the shift to new staples invariably produced periods of crises in which adjustments in the old structure were painfully made, and a new pattern created in relation to a new staple." However, Innis displays a "deep-founded and ongoing skepticism about markets as a universal mechanism of well-being" (Drache 1995, li). Instead, he advocates "to study actual economic life" (xix), and he explicitly calls for state intervention to preserve "long-term stability and economic security" (li). Hence, with a new organizing mechanism, adjustments in the old structure have to be painfully made, but Innis sees it as the task of governance to mitigate the painfulness. McLuhan's surprisingly applied and interventionist side sounds like this: quoting the biologist John Z. Young with the statement that "great changes in ways of ordinary human speaking and acting are bound up with the adoption of new instruments," McLuhan ([1962] 2002, 6) grumbles, "Had we meditated on such a basic fact as that long ago, we might easily have mastered the nature and effects of all our technologies, instead of being pushed around by them." Hence McLuhan deems it possible to *master* technologies rather than just being exposed to their effects, but it demands great efforts at the cultivation of "critical habits of mind" (Pooley 2016). Therefore, resting on the classic theme of critical theory, the good organization by and of media should not be left to market mechanisms alone.

Geert Lovink and Ned Rossiter argue for "a passionate pragmatism to define and shape the architecture of new media" (Lovink 2012, 1). Lovink reflects on this move "into practicality" as follows: having practiced "postmodern metaphysics, 'deep irrelevance' European style," himself for years, he started to miss acting toward a political framework. "I experienced a lack of strategy amongst cultural critics who were unable to effectively do something against the hegemony of global neo-liberalism" (4). Underpinning this, the first sentence of Rossiter's book reads, "There is an urgent need for new institutional forms." According to him, encompassing computer networks have produced "uncertainties of labour and life" that are exposing "the limits of prevailing institutional systems" (Rossiter 2006, 13). Reminding of Innis, he claims that to "recompose labour and life in ways that furnish a sense of security and stability," it is necessary to organize the new sociotechnical configurations, meaning to make an intervention and to "attend to the task of governance" (17).

What does it mean to attend to the task of governance? In the afterword of their recent publication *Organization after Social Media* (and echoed in the afterword of this volume), Rossiter and Lovink lament the lack of organizedness among the Left manifested by its exceptional "downward trajectory." They ask, "How has populist politics organized as movements, while the radical left seems as incapable as ever to crystalize a collective imaginary that is in sync with the current social media condition?" To them, attending to the task of governance—or at least articulating one's voice with regard to governance—seems to be related to finding a form that corresponds to the technological environment. One example for this correspondence they give is the "umbrella movement" sparking in Hong Kong in 2014. Using an off-the-grid Bluetooth network (FireChat), the protesters were able to communicate among each other—and to organize themselves—without having been dependent on an internet connection and without having fueled the police's database. Such a distributed media practice troubles the centralizing, aggregating, and correlating use of network media by those in power while still making use of networks. Also, Lovink and Rossiter (2018, 3) suggest that strong ties and long commitments are needed in a technoculture that works precisely against them. But how can this be achieved—"the organization of passions that endure"? What are networks organized in a way that they are capable of making decisions, taking action, and making a long-term difference? Does an answer lie with think tank like "secret societies"? If the internet actually resembles a schoolyard where people hang out, chat, and harass each other, then a way to balance these tendencies could indeed be more organization as we learned it from clubs, associations, unions, or bureaucracy.

Last, and thus coming back to the beginning, what does the wobbly question of "the good organization" mean for the case of ERP software? How do the "adjustments painfully made" manifest themselves? How could they be eased for the sake of "security and stability"? What comes to mind are the frequent stories of SAP introductions not turning out as intended (e.g., Westelius 2006; Ciborra 2000). This means the implementation of the software package leads to significant organizational chaos, in extreme cases causing temporary shutdowns or even the cancellation of the implementation project. The most recent story comes from the German discount grocer Lidl. In July 2018, Lidl stopped the introduction of SAP HANA/Retail after seven years of development and 500 million euros of investment. Apparently, what had led to this development was the well-known conflict between software customization, on one hand, and organizational reengineering, on the other hand. SAP offers a standard software that works best if the company adapts its processes to the software. Customizing the software so as to accommodate a company's existing processes makes it more complex, more expensive, less stable, and less reliable. The latter is said to have happened to Lidl. It commissioned wide-ranging changes to the software unprepared to transform its own structures. In the end, the software was not performing well, while the costs continued to rise (Kolf and Kerkmann 2018).

Extensively covered by industrial sociology, there are also stories of individual employment biographies being disrupted by new technologies and the competences it demands, or rather, the competences it renders obsolete. In this sense, a new ERP software terminates preceding and often well-established actor-networks. For instance, Becker, Vering, and Winkelmann (2007, 202) report on certain sectors running entirely on systems without graphical user interface, hence they are handled only via keyboard. In interaction with these systems, the employees had learned to work "blindly," meaning they relied on the beeps and thereby achieved high speed. With a new system, such a skill becomes worthless. In situations like these, and depending on their age, employees prefer (or are encouraged) to leave their jobs instead of acquiring the skills necessary for the new generation of software. This is certainly also a fear the interviewee Mrs. J. had when the introduction of SAP was announced. But she took on the self-understanding of being an eager and lifelong learner. Something new again, but it will be feasible. When I talked to her two years later, she was in full control of the SAP system. Even more, she realized that the system would produce "total chaos" if she did not correct it constantly. These corrections were based on her experiential knowledge of working at company N. for twenty years. Thus, in adjusting the system, she continued to be valuable to the company.

How do media and organization relate to each other? In this text, I gathered arguments from media studies, organization studies, and neighboring streams of research and complemented them with the case of business software, an exemplary case of gray media. In doing so, three ways of drafting the relation between media and organization appeared. The first one bears upon the proposition that "media organize" (Martin 2003), and it explores media in terms of their organizing capacities. The second line of inquiry complicated the first one by pointing to the organizedness of media. It revolves around media's entanglement with institutional cultures and broader technological environments. Last, a normative question arose: media organize and media are organized, but what does it mean for them to be organized *well*? I outlined some of the research efforts addressing this question.

In September 2018, the founding conference of the Munich Center for Emancipatory Technology Studies took place. Speakers from science, politics, unions, and civil society investigate ways of governing technology that aim at "good jobs, lived democracy, a self-governed life and ecological sustainability" (Zentrum emanzipatorische Technikforschung 2018). At this point, the ghost of Kittler could be summoned to undermine all efforts of realizing a good organization of media based on thoroughly understanding their nature and their effects. "Understanding media," Kittler (1999, xl) has written, "remains an impossibility precisely because the dominant information technologies of the day control all understanding and its illusions." But then again, why not summon another authority in response encouraging us to attempt "the art of not being governed quite so much" (Foucault 2007, 45)?

Notes

1   It was part of fieldwork I conducted at the medium-sized metalworking business N. between 2012 and 2015. Publications based on this fieldwork are Conrad (2017, forthcoming-a, forthcoming-b).

2   Siegele and Zeppelin quote from Werner Sombart's "Der moderne Kapitalis-

mus": "One plainly cannot think capitalism without double-entry bookkeeping: they relate to each other like form and content" (Sombart [1917] 2012, 118, translation by the author).

3 This calls for a definition of organizing: What kinds of actions does this term refer to? What is not-organizing? I am not sure there is a satisfying answer to this. In organization studies, to talk of organizing instead of organization(s) implies being part of the process philosophy school of thought that criticizes the discipline's occupation with organizations as entities. Representatives say that "to organize is a process, whether it is a matter of fixing a door, writing a letter or restructuring a large corporation. It does not really matter in terms of analysis whether we fix a door or restructure a corporation" (Hernes 2008, xvi–xvii). Today organization studies is a thoroughly interdisciplinary field without a consensus about its area of competence. Scholars deal with a barely sortable range of phenomena and concepts (cf. Hernes 2008, 147–48). On the undisciplined, creole, pidgin, and bazaar-ish character of organization studies, see also Czarniawska (2003) and Beyes (2007).

4 "Humble tools," or gray media, are also addressed in Joanne Yates's research in business history. She attributes a crucial role to them: "From the U.S. Postal Service to typewriters, vertical files, and adding machines, technologies and techniques of information gathering, storage, manipulation, and communication have figured prominently in the evolution of firms and business practices" (Yates 2005, 1).

5 These tools can be shiny and innovative or ordinary, unremarkable, and infrastructural. This depends on the degree of newness ascribed to them and the degree of familiarity acquired with regard to them (Edwards 2003, 185).

6 In this phase, Innis conducted what has later been called "dirt research": in a kayak, he traveled the country westward along the continent's interlocking lake and river systems and gathered all kinds of information related to staple production (cf. Creighton 1957, 49–60; Rossiter 2012).

7 Today an understanding of landscape as material power can also be found in cultural geography, for instance, in Mitchell's (2002) *Landscape and Power.*

8 In this chapter, Wiener basically describes the possibility of teleportation. Because he assumes a human being (an individuality) to be constituted by certain patterns of information (generated through past development and continued development along these lines), he deduces that "there is no absolute distinction between the types of transmission which we can use for sending a telegram from country to country and the types of transmission which at least are theoretically possible for transmitting a living organism such as a human being" (Wiener [1950] 1989, 103).

9 Herman Hollerith's Tabulating Machine Company (1896) merged into the International Business Machines Corporation (IBM) in 1924.

10 "The Good Organization" was the general theme of the 2017 colloquium of the European Group for Organizational Studies (EGOS). It revolved around the notion that organization could be "a force for the greater good, public as well as private," while being reflexive about the history and normativity of this idea.

References

Becker, Jörg, Oliver Vering, and Axel Winkelmann. 2007. *Softwareauswahl und -einführung in Industrie und Handel: Vorgehen bei und Erfahrungen mit ERP- und Warenwirtschaftssystemen.* Heidelberg, Germany: Springer.

Beyes, Timon. 2007. "Organisationstheorien von Agamben bis Žižek. Auf dem Basar der Organization Studies." In *Fokus Organisation: Sozialwissenschaftliche Perspektiven und Analysen,* edited by Thomas Eberle, Sabine Hoidn, and Katarina Sikavica, 65–86. Konstanz, Germany: UVK.

Campbell-Kelly, Martin. 1992. "Large-Scale Data Processing in the Prudential, 1850–1930." *Accounting, Business, and Financial History* 2, no. 2: 117–40.

Ciborra, Claudio U., ed. 2000. *From Control to Drift: The Dynamics of Corporate Information Infrastructures.* Oxford: Oxford University Press.

Conrad, Lisa. 2017. *Organisation im soziotechnischen Gemenge: Mediale Umschichtungen durch die Einführung von SAP.* Bielefeld, Germany: transcript.

Conrad, Lisa. Forthcoming-a. "The Organization Is a Repair Shop." *ephemera: theory and politics in organization* 19, no. 2: 303–24.

Conrad, Lisa. Forthcoming-b. "Planning Table." In *The Oxford Handbook of Media, Technology and Organisation,* edited by Timon Beyes, Robin Holt, and Claus Pias. Oxford: Oxford University Press.

Creighton, Donald. 1957. *Harold Innis: Portrait of a Scholar.* Toronto: Toronto University Press.

Czarniawska, Barbara. 2003. "This Way to Paradise: On Creole Researchers, Hybrid Disciplines, and Pidgin Writing." *Organization* 10, no. 3: 430–34.

de Laet, Marianne, and Annemarie Mol. 2000. "The Zimbabwe Bush Pump: Mechanics of a Fluid Technology." *Social Studies of Science* 30, no. 2: 225–63.

Dommann, Monika. 2014. *Autoren und Apparate: Die Geschichte des Copyrights im Medienwandel.* Frankfurt am Main, Germany: S. Fischer.

Drache, Daniel. 1995. "Celebrating Innis: The Man, the Legacy, and Our Future." In *Staples, Markets, and Cultural Change: Selected Essays,* edited by Harold Adam Innis, xiii–lix. Montreal: McGill-Queen's University Press.

Edwards, Paul N. 2003. "Infrastructure and Modernity: Force, Time, and Social Organization in the History of Sociotechnical Systems." In *Modernity and Technology,* edited by Thomas J. Misa, Philip Brey, and Andrew Feenberg, 185–225. Cambridge, Mass.: MIT Press.

Foucault, Michel. 2007. *The Politics of Truth.* Los Angeles, Calif.: Semiotext(e).

Fuller, Mathew, and Andrew Goffey. 2012. *Evil Media.* Cambridge, Mass.: MIT Press.

Gitelman, Lisa. 2014. *Paper Knowledge: Toward a Media History of Documents.* Durham, N.C.: Duke University Press.

Hagner, Michael, and Erich Hörl, eds. 2008. *Die Transformation des Humanen: Beiträge zur Kulturgeschichte der Kybernetik.* Frankfurt am Main, Germany: Suhrkamp.

Heide, Lars. 2009. *Punched-Card Systems and the Early Information Explosion, 1880–1945.* Baltimore, Md.: Johns Hopkins University Press.

Hernes, Tor. 2008. *Understanding Organization as Process: Theory for a Tangled World.* London: Routledge.

Hörl, Erich. 2016. "Erich Hörl: A Continent Inter-view." *continent* 5, no. 2: 25–30.

Horn, Eva. 2007. "Editor's Introduction: 'There Are No Media.'" *Grey Room* 29: 6–13.

Hull, Matthew S. 2012. "Documents and Bureaucracy." *Annual Review of Anthropology* 41: 251–67.

Innis, Harold A. 1923. *A History of the Canadian Pacific Railway.* Toronto: University of Toronto Press.

Innis, Harold A. 1930. *The Fur Trade in Canada: An Introduction to Canadian Economic History.* Toronto: University of Toronto Press.

Innis, Harold A. 1940. *The Cod Fisheries: The History of an International Economy.* Toronto: Ryerson Press.

Innis, Harold A. 1950. *Empire and Communications.* Victoria, Sask.: Press Porcépic.

Kafka, Ben. 2012. *The Demon of Writing: Powers and Failures of Paperwork.* New York: Zone Books.

Katz, Elihu. 1987. "Communications Research since Lazarsfeld." *Public Opinion Quarterly* 51 no. 4/2: 25–45.

Kittler, Friedrich. 1999. *Gramophone, Film, Typewriter.* Stanford, Calif.: Stanford University Press.

Kline, Ronald R. 2015. *The Cybernetics Moment; or, Why We Call Our Age the Information Age.* Baltimore, Md.: Johns Hopkins University Press.

Kolf, Florian, and Christof Kerkmann. 2018. "Lidl software disaster another example of Germany's digital failure." *Handelsblatt Global,* July 30. https://global.handels blatt.com/companies/lidl-software-flop-germany-digital-failure-950223.

Larkin, Brian. 2004. "Degraded Images, Distorted Sounds: Nigerian Video and the Infrastructure of Piracy." *Public Culture* 16, no. 2: 289–314.

Latour, Bruno. 2013. "'What's the Story?' Organizing as a Mode of Existence." In *Organization and Organizing: Materiality, Agency and Discourse,* edited by Daniel Robichaud and François Cooren, 37–51. London: Routledge.

Lovink, Geert. 2012. "The Art of Electronic Dialogue: A Self-Interview: Introduction to Uncanny Networks." *kunsttexte.de* 3: 1–5.

Lovink, Geert, and Ned Rossiter. 2018. *Organization after Social Media.* Colchester, U.K.: Minor Compositions.

Martin, Reinhold. 2003. *The Organizational Complex: Architecture, Media, and Corporate Space.* Cambridge, Mass.: MIT Press.

McLuhan, Marshall. (1962) 2002. *The Gutenberg Galaxy: The Making of Typographic Man.* Toronto: Toronto University Press.

McLuhan, Marshall. (1964) 1994. *Understanding Media: The Extensions of Man.* Cambridge, Mass.: MIT Press.

Medina, Eden. 2011. *Cybernetic Revolutionaries: Technology and Politics in Allende's Chile.* Cambridge, Mass.: MIT Press.

Mitchell, W. J. T., ed. 2002. *Landscape and Power: Space, Place, and Landscape.* Chicago: University of Chicago Press.

Mormann, Hannah. 2016. *Das Projekt SAP: Zur Organisationssoziologie betriebswirtschaftlicher Software.* Bielefeld, Germany: transcript.

Orlikowski, Wanda, and C. Suzanne Iacono. 2001. "Research Commentary:

Desperately Seeking the 'IT' in IT Research—a Call to Theorizing the IT Artifact." *Information Systems Research* 12, no. 2: 121–34.

Orlikowski, Wanda J., and Susan V. Scott. 2008. "Sociomateriality: Challenging the Separation of Technology, Work and Organization." *Academy of Management Annals* 2, no. 1: 433–74.

Peters, Ben. 2016. *How Not to Network a Nation: The Uneasy History of the Soviet Internet.* Cambridge, Mass.: MIT Press.

Peters, John Durham. 2015. *The Marvelous Clouds: Toward a Philosophy of Elemental Media.* Chicago: University of Chicago Press.

Pias, Claus, ed. 2003. *Cybernetics—Kybernetik: The Macy-Conferences 1946–1953.* Zurich: Diaphanes.

Pollock, Neil, and Robin Williams. 2009. *Software and Organisations: The Biography of the Enterprise-Wide System or How SAP Conquered the World.* London: Routledge.

Pollock, Neil, Robin Williams, and Luciana D'Adderio. 2007. "Global Software and Its Provenance: Generification Work in the Production of Organizational Software Packages." *Social Studies of Science* 37, no. 2: 254–80.

Pooley, Jefferson. 2016. "How to Become a Famous Media Scholar: The Case of Marshall McLuhan." *Los Angeles Review of Books,* December.

Quattrone, Paolo, and François-Régís Puyou. Forthcoming. "Account Book." In *The Oxford Handbook of Media, Technology, and Organization Studies,* edited by Timon Beyes, Robin Holt, and Claus Pias. Oxford: Oxford University Press.

Rheinberger, Hans-Jörg. 1997. *Toward a History of Epistemic Things: Synthesizing Protein in the Test Tube.* Stanford, Calif.: Stanford University Press.

Rossiter, Ned. 2006. *Organized Networks: Media Theory, Creative Labour, New Institutions.* Rotterdam, Netherlands: NAi.

Rossiter, Ned. 2012. "Dirt Research." In *Depletion Design: A Glossary of Network Ecology,* edited by Carolin Wiedemann and Sönke Zehle, 41–45. Amsterdam: XMLab/Institute for Network Cultures.

Siegele, Ludwig, and Joachim Zepelin. 2009. *Matrix der Welt: SAP und der neue globale Kapitalismus.* Frankfurt am Main, Germany: Campus.

Siegert, Bernhard. 1999. *Relays: Literature as an Epoch of the Postal System.* Stanford, Calif.: Stanford University Press.

Siegert, Bernhard. 2006. *Passagiere und Papiere: Schreibakte auf der Schwelle zwischen Spanien und Amerika.* Munich: Wilhelm Fink.

Sombart, Werner. (1917) 2012. *Der moderne Kapitalismus: Historisch-systematische Darstellung des gesamteuropäischen Wirtschaftslebens von seinen Anfängen bis zur Gegenwart.* Paderborn, Germany: Salzwasser.

Star, Susan Leigh, and Geoffrey C. Bowker. 2002. *Sorting Things Out: Classification and Its Consequences.* Cambridge, Mass.: MIT Press.

Star, Susan Leigh, and Martha Lampland. 2009. *Standards and Their Stories: How Quantifying, Classifying, and Formalizing Practices Shape Everyday Life.* Ithaca, N.Y.: Cornell University Press.

Tenen, Dennis. 2017. *Plain Text: The Poetics of Computation.* Stanford, Calif.: Stanford University Press.

Vismann, Cornelia. 2008. *Files: Law and Media Technology.* Stanford, Calif.: Stanford University Press.

Vogl, Joseph. 2007. "Becoming-Media: Galileo's Telescope." *Grey Room* 29: 14–25.

Westelius, Alf. 2006: "Muddling Through: The Life of a Multinational, Strategic Enterprise Systems Venture at BT Industries." *Linköping Electronic Articles in Computer and Information Science* 10, no. 1: 1–46.

Wiener, Norbert. (1950) 1989. *The Human Use of Human Beings: Cybernetics and Society.* London: Free Association Books.

Yates, Joanne. 1993. "Co-evolution of Information-Processing Technology and Use: Interaction between the Life Insurance and Tabulating Industries." *Business History Review* 67, no. 1: 1–51.

Yates, Joanne. 1999. "The Structuring of Early Computer Use in Life Insurance." *Journal of Design History* 12, no. 1: 5–24

Yates, Joanne. 2000. "Business Use of Information and Technology during the Industrial Age." In *A Nation Transformed by Information,* edited by Alfred D. Chandler Jr. and James W. Cortada, 107–36. Oxford: Oxford University Press.

Yates, Joanne. 2005. *Structuring the Information Age: Life Insurance and Technology in the Twentieth Century.* Baltimore, Md.: Johns Hopkins University Press.

Zentrum emanzipatorische Technikforschung. 2018. *Technikpolitik von unten: Digitalisierung, Gewerkschaft, Emanzipation.* Founding conference, September 7–8. https://emancipatory.technology/konferenz/.

Zuboff, Shoshonna. 1988. *In the Age of the Smart Machine.* New York: Basic Books.

Afterword

Propositions on the Organizational Form

Geert Lovink and Ned Rossiter

Media and Organization

The quest of organization haunts us. If anarchists were once said to defy authority, nowadays we defy organization. Structures are perceived to hold us back and pin us down with the iron cage of identity. The solidified social limits our freedom with its demand of never-ending "engagement." How desperate is it to live your life as an insulated rebel without a cause? Instead, we should ask, what is pure organization? Is there a new core that we could define and design? What's commitment outside of today's technosocial conventions? Are there bonds that create ties, unhinged from procedure, unfettered by bureaucracy? Is there a form of conspiracy that operates without all the tiresome preparations? Mutual aid and local self-organization come to mind, but what if we're forced to pursue organization of the unorganizables? Does a self-evident General Will exist that does not need to be discussed and exhaustively questioned? Having arrived at this point, we can clearly see the romantic undertone of the Critique of Organization. What's a lean revolution, an effortless regime change? Can we presuppose a hive mind that performs like an automaton? Humans, coming together, create the Event, simply because of an inner urge to experience relations without guarantees.

What does organization mean in a culture of shrinking commitment? Nowadays, the decision to commit is one made after a cost–benefit analysis. Options are kept alive as possibilities of transactions with higher returns. Everyday life, as Randy Martin (2002) so insightfully analyzed, is infused with financialization. Intimacy now bears the cold face of nihilism. Once life is unburdened of fixed dates and routine tasks, the horizon of choice fuels the desire to defer any obligation. This is the logical extension of post-Fordist labor regimes predicated on flexibility without a future. A social desert blooms in the techno-abyss of weak ties.

What are the prevailing forces, conditions, and events that galvanize organization, as distinct from disorganization, entropy, indifference, flexibilization, or outbursts without an agenda? Reinhold Martin's concept "media organize" is a key injunction in this book on organization. For Martin, media are defined by their organizational function: media organize. At the core of this thesis is the production of order that generates patterns and relations. Constituted through material properties and the partitioning work of form, the order of media is a way of distinguishing different organizational dynamics and forces. Similarly, organizational tendencies, practices, and capacities become a way to define media and distinguish one medium from another. Organization is coupled with form. The question of organization for us has, for many years, been key to political design within a world of persistent crisis, struggle, even chaos. What governs in a world in which the ordering work of government is in near-total disrepute?

The Cambridge Analytica controversy of early 2018 prompts us to ask, first, whether geopolitical forces condition or organize media to organize. Cambridge Analytica–Facebook very deliberately decided to touch down in the United States as the primary test-bed; the rest of the world was not so relevant. They are part of the larger FANG "plat-formatting" of economy and society (Mackenzie and Munster 2019), along with TenCent, Baidu, and the Chinese logistical media juggernaut. In this regard, media do indeed organize. However, it is not really possible to return to the media format as we have known it during the era of broadcast communications. Is the platform itself the core of the problem or part of the solution? There is a post-Hegelian dilemma here: what comes after the synthesis? Usually implosion and collapse. No apotheosis. What are the counterforces that can challenge the platform? The federation of decentralized platforms? Post-platform—is that all there is? It might be premature to answer these questions. It's early days for the platform as form.

In the wake of Cambridge Analytica–Facebook, we find ourselves asking what's organization after social media? We can trawl through the Marx–Bakunin–Lenin debates, even read them on repeat mode in the "Jodi Dean" retro style that wants to make the American Communist Party Great Again, but there is no point in re-cuperating the worn-out organs of the party. Another option is the party–movement hybrid, a party of parties, a federation of political entities, which was extensively discussed in the context of Syriza, Podemos, and DiEM25, each an initiative that came out of the 2011 uprisings. A leap-frogging of technomodernity happened when enough noise gathered around the squares, from the Arab Spring, via WikiLeaks and Anonymous, to Black Lives Matter and #MeToo, which makes one think that yes, maybe social media do indeed organize. But organize what? Those "early" years, not even a decade ago, situated organization as a media event that facilitates consciousness raising and acts as a tool for pressure groups and lobbyists to turn the party into something with social momentum. But the revolution never happened. And it never will. The scale of crisis has shown that no amount of coalition building among nations will fix the living hell of the future-present. The corporate-run nation-state does not offer any solutions either. This is why so much of the political energy these days is focused on the municipal level, including city-to-city networks (Caccia 2016).

Let's hear more about the Protestant colleges before they became absorbed into the military–industrial–educational complex. And what about Norman Foster's new Apple campus in Cupertino, California? How has that complex devoted energies and decision-making to transform the organizational logic and production of knowledge and subjectivity? Will it be an organizational model rolled out elsewhere across the world, like the glass-and-steel skyscrapers were in the twentieth century? We fully agree that architecture mediates and organizes the world to which it refers. What would happen if we were to run architecture-as-media alongside networks-as-organization? Architecture as a complex of social relations, infrastructural capacities, engineering standards, and aesthetic styles distinguished the mode of organization in the nineteenth and twentieth centuries. This set of protocols has not gone away but is now complemented by architecture as a computational parameter in the modeling of algorithmic governance tasked with prediction and preemption coupled with the extraction and amplified abstraction of data from the toils of labor and the social production of value.

If we are to think organization in relation to networks (power laws, scale-free networks, weak ties vs. strong ties), then our focus might be directed toward post-platform media—what are the media of organized networks defined by strong ties, and what is it about their properties that engenders particular organizational tendencies? Indeed, do media matter within postdigital conditions when environment is increasingly understood as the background mediating system through which communication is signaled and relations are forged? Environment organizes as media slip away.

Inevitable Incorporations

Recent decades are defined by a complete upending of modern models of organization. Indeed, there has been a breakdown of traditional organizations. Political activists, movements, and theorists (from cybernetics to post-humanism) are dogged by disorganization as the dominant condition. The entrepreneurial monopolies don't mind this at all. They work out how to siphon data and wash it with a magic wand that spits out value.

How to understand organization in times of neoliberal clouds, personalized networks, and advanced forms of non-commitment? The performance and management of work are, in fact, highly organized, yet require of workers some sort of antiwork attitude. Tasks are not just routines. Sure, there is TaskRabbit, and there's no doubt that freelancers find a routine in the struggle to make some coin. But, like Amazon Mechanical Turk, the key task here is to ensure that the human is no longer distinct from the machine. Traditionally, routines would vary over the course of the day or change in season. By contrast, the task of the machine is to never end, just keep chugging along and, ideally, accelerating as time elapses.

Universities are heading in the same direction, where much that used to be understood as *Bildung* is now an exercise in automation. As Stefano Harney notes, in the algorithmic institution, "most managers have already been replaced by machines. They are just too dumb to know it" (Schapira and Montgomery 2017). According to Harney,

> the consultant is nothing more than a demonstration of access. He or she can show up in your workplace and open it up in ways you thought were protected, solid. His presence is proof that you are now newly accessible. No one needs to listen to a consultant. He is just a talking algorithm anyway. But he has made his point by showing up.

Organization needs to exit the innocence of immanent planes, endless assemblages, and the allocation of distinct tasks and management of issues. Organization also offers us a parallel world to the constant highs and lows of our not so private lives and states of mind. The managerial discourse of fluidity is rampant across institutional settings within advanced economies and defines the culture of organization disconnected from the world to which it refers. There is no backup plan for the unbearable lightness of commitment. Organization within conditions of contemporary media will need to devise strategies alert to the parameters of platforms and apps that shape perception and cognition. What happens when contract workers walk away from the job but categorically deny they are on strike? Why does such a profound depoliticization encapsulate such acts of refusal? How has this come to be understood as another lifestyle option rather than some collective instantiation of shared experience that demands revolt? The end of the contract is not internalized as the humility of being fired; rather, dignity upholds the narrative of legitimate existence within a managerial paradigm that work, similar to life, has a beginning, middle, and end. As much as vulnerability is a common condition, it cannot be named as such because it violates the self-invested code of liberty that props up portfolio careers. Atomization is one of the core problems for organization within situations defined by platform participation.

Herein lies the predicament. If you are not the cool kid hooked on the delusion of entrepreneurial self-invention, where are you other than cast adrift, gravitating toward the ugly sentiments of populist politics that define the alt-right and similar formations? How has populist politics organized as movements, while the radical Left seems as incapable as ever to crystalize a collective imaginary that is in sync with the current social media condition? How to get rid of all these real existing resentments? How can alt-right be sabotaged and denied access to the collective unconscious of today's potential rebel forces? Fast updating, ever-changing timelines, snappy and dark comment culture—this is the grammar of media that is not about having dialogues, debating issues, or sharing material but rather dominated by motives such as trawling, shitstorm, anger, aggression, frustration, and despair. These are the core elements of the social media condition. Habermas's idealized public sphere is nowhere to be found in this environment of terminated futures. Alt-right is not at all marginal (and faces its own organizational problems) but in fact occupies the space of the new norm. The access to power through Breitbart and similar platforms is, these days, very different from the logic of representational media that

mirrored the old corridors of power with its think tanks, consul-
tants, lobby groups, and political parties. The networked media
of platforms that attract and then agglomerate social disaffection
are able to mainline the people to the figureheads of power. This
is why Trump, for instance, has been able to maintain such high
approval ratings despite the disoriented Left in the United States
puzzling over their failure to extend the path to glory.

Think Tank Theory

How can we imagine doing radical research outside of the established academic institutions and large mainstream media? Is this
possible anyway? Social movements have always undertaken their
own research, comparable to political parties and their "scientific
offices." These days, NGOs produce tons of reports. Up until the
1990s, this work was imagined as an intellectual practice allocated
deep inside the social movements themselves. The work mostly
comprised investigative journalism, activist research into corporations, mapping extreme-right-wing networks and organizations,
nuclear energy deals, and related lobby campaigns of multination-
als that supported the apartheid regime in South Africa. This type
of "indy research" was done to inform the movements themselves
and provide them with info-ammunition in the fight for the hearts
and minds of the people (sometimes confused by many with "public opinion").

If we consider Amsterdam in the 1980s, we find a blossoming of
research undertaken by groups of the nonaligned. There were
separate autonomous research collectives that monitored racists
and neofascists (FOK), a group that followed police and secret
service activities (Jansen & Jansen), an outfit that investigated
speculation and gentrification in the city (SPOK), and even a theory
and humanities arm of the squatters movement (ADILKNO/Agentur
Bilwet). In some instances, the groups were linked to specific archives or magazines, as was the case with radical feminism. The
last thing these research collectives wanted to do was to produce
dull policy papers.

None of these groups used the corporate term *think tank* or *scientific bureau* (attached to a political party), even though that's arguably what they were. Perhaps it was enough to be in a collective? But in these terms, there is no explicit connection with thinking. The pondering time of thinking didn't seem to be very sexy (that was something associated with the sequestered and therefore apolitical work of scholars); neither was collective research considered to be situating your group inside a tank. But, then, why call yourself a foundation (a legal term, controlled by lawyers and notaries), or an institute, for that matter, the very symbol of one's desire to be part of official reality and its "institutionalization"? NGOs were also on the radar back then, although they were associated with the United Nations and de facto ministries of the state. Often enough, their "non" was, and still is, a farce.

Over the past decade, the Better Think Tank Project (BTTP) of the Munich art duo Ralf Homann and Manuela Unverdorben has looked at the issue of think tanks from an artistic perspective. The duo investigates the politics and aesthetics of think tanks as a dominant form of knowledge production. What's the appeal of the motor behind the current innovation madness? Are think tanks deadly boring? What do we gain from a copy-and-paste of these kind of forms other than mimicking their sociospatial culture (such as "the office")? We asked the duo why there aren't any leftist think tanks (Lovink 2018): "When the entrepreneur Anthony Fisher wanted to use his fortune to influence British politics and asked Friedrich von Hayek which party to support, he got the hint not to waste time and gain instead decisive influence in the battle of ideas by funding research in structural forms like think tanks. Think tanks are a better tool to persist the myth of an objective truth."

Their responses are worth reading at length: "It's a common misunderstanding that think tanks are actually creative units, let alone were established with this intention. Think tanks label themselves 'independent' but still push their backer's agenda and accomplish credibility by pretending to be neutral and to conduct serious research. However, instead of actual academic research

they operate as echo chambers, multiplicators of the neoliberal
ideological agenda. There is no real eagerness in thinking up new
ideas, because they already possess the 'truth.' Instead, they aim
to influence public opinion, to intervene in policy-making and to
spread their program."

The Munich simulation duo are all fired up: "To dance at the
Capitalist Ball is a lot of fun! But be beware of misunderstandings.
If it should happen that the think tank dress code would change
to hoodies then we also would reflect on that. Still, we watch the
developments in the NGO field critically, especially when NGOs are
acting as think tanks. Progressive movements should be based on
solidarity and organizational forms of solidarity."

Since 2005, we have been working together on the idea of "organized networks." Recently, we brought together our writings in a
book called *Organization after Social Media* (2018). Radical think tank
theory can be considered a contribution to this project, albeit from
the opposite direction, as think tanks are usually allocated to the
space of bricks and mortar. Organized networks, by contrast, are
tight virtual networks, defined by their "strong ties," with dispersed
contributors that do without expensive office spaces. However,
what organized networks and think tanks have in common is a commitment to be there for the long haul. Such a proposal is anathema
to the brave "orgnet" comrades condemned to spend their days in
coworking spaces, in cafés, and at home at the kitchen table. How
did we end up in such a neoliberal trap? How can we transform that
temporary precarious work into a long-term sustainable project
without falling into the NGO predicament? We urgently need new
forms and cultural imaginaries to conspire. One of the many ways
to get there is through the deconstruction of hegemonic formats.
How can we envision the radical or post–think tank as a form?

Writing from Milan via email, Alex Foti (pers. comm., May 10, 2018)
reports on his latest initiative to set up a think tank and explains his
motivation to use this particular term and organizational format.
"Nick Srnicek and others highlighted the role of the Mont Pelerin

Society in establishing neoliberal orthodoxy from the fringes by means of think tanking. While we cannot forego an analysis of the revolutionary subject, which in my opinion is the precariat, it is true that all forms of the Left are at a historical low (certainly in Europe). We need an intellectual strategy to rebuild values and ideology and wage successful battles against oligopolistic capital and win the mortal combat with nazi-populism from Washington to Ankara. Closer to our Milanese reality, we are witnessing a conservative return to old Marxist–Leninist certainties even among young sections of the movement, and a concomitant renewed emphasis on work and the working class at the expense of universal basic income and the polygendered, multiethnic precariat. The idea is to merge the intellectual curiosity of today's student movement with cognitarians from previous waves of protest (2001 and 2010 in Italy). The name of our think tank is still tentative as we have only gathered informally, but I like best ALIEN INTELLIGENCE: The Post-capitalist Exoplanet."

Whether think tanks are the most strategic radical form to chime with our times remains to be seen. We need examples to bounce around our ideas and concepts. Hit-and-run actions that result in loose coalitions falling apart once the event is over should no longer be encouraged, if not straight out rejected. Think tanks are worth exploring and experimenting with to see whether a leftist politics can be designed within what historically has been an alien machine. Put bluntly, the downward trajectory of the Left has reached a point where there is no option: invent new organizational and institutional forms or inhabit and remake existing ones. Unless the Left gets serious about this, it will only further consign itself to irrelevance as the planet endures prolonged crisis.

Sovereign Media and the Organization of Emptiness

The current economy of sharing and the business of data extractivism are the key techniques of contemporary platform capitalism

(Srnicek 2017), which only goes so far as a concept or model of media and organization. Lacking nuance and bound to the logic of expropriation, the narrow spectrum of platform capitalism is less about dominant social media networks than it is about the total lack of sovereignty, dignity, and empathy as a mentality, self-image, and survival tactic to overcome technonihilism and its unconscious maneuvers that steer and capture the online self. There's something rich and intriguing about standing up and taking back one's information destiny. This is what we call *sovereign media,* a declaration and act of creating autonomous data and network infrastructures. Such interventions go beyond occasional radical gestures and the spectacle of the event.

Sovereign media configure territory and power in a world thoroughly enmeshed with media systems and technological agents. The underlying technics of media platforms also bear upon the production of subjectivity, organizing perception, cognition, and sociality in ways that unsettle and reorient modern understandings of the primary organizational forms that govern labor and life (the church, state, firm, union). But this unsettling of dominant organizational forms is also a productive process. "Organization is the central and basic material element of the constitution of the subject" (Negri 2005, 147). There's a latent formalist tendency within the dictum "media organize." Let us not forget that media also organize subjects, and the struggle that underpins such a process is the work of politics and the political.

As negative technologies without a megaphone, sovereign media disappear into the sea of noise. They are subtractive machines, clawing back "data assets" from centers of control. A great example here is the use of off-the-grid Bluetooth networks as the primary technique of organization for the umbrella movement in Hong Kong. This distributed mode of communication during the 2014 occupation and summer of skirmishes ensured the absence of a centralized archive for the surveillance machine of authorities. Denied the capacity to correlate information and generate a data universe of the movement, authorities instead had to infiltrate the many gatherings and actions in the hope of compiling partial personas of rebels with a cause. Such instances in which total knowledge is disabled as a result of distributed forms of communication also register an epistemological crisis. This is the crisis of neopositivism, which has undergone a resurgence over the past decade as new quantitative techniques have emerged with the advent of big data analytics. Long weary of the critical lessons of post-structuralism, the humanities and social sciences have embraced neopositivism to legitimize claims of knowledge. Not only, then, does the mode of communication adopted by the umbrella movement instruct us about how to organize in strategic ways that trouble, if not undermine, contemporary techniques of policing, but it also signals a more substantive crisis that pertains to how the world is known, how subjects are produced, and, subsequently, how politics is organized.

In asking the question how media organize politics and subjectivity, we must take care not to be distracted by the seduction of reproduction. To do so would be a fatal political and conceptual mistake. What is clear from the history of movements is the medium specificity of their emergence. Whether it is pamphlets or fax machines, videos or mobile phones, Twitter or Facebook, political organization is always technological but also social and historical. The audacity of insurrection is made possible by media of organization tied to the organization of passions that endure.

References

Caccia, Beppe. 2016. "A European Network of Rebel Cities?" Open Democracy, June 5. https://www.opendemocracy.net/can-europe-make-it/beppe-caccia/european -network-of-rebel-cities.

Lovink, Geert. 2018. "Radical Think-Tank Theory: Interview with Ralf Homann and Manuela Unverdorben." Nettime (mailing list), April 19. https://nettime.org/ Lists-Archives/nettime-l-1804/msg00071.html.

Lovink, Geert, and Ned Rossiter. 2018. *Organization after Social Media.* Colchester, U.K.: Minor Compositions/Autonomedia.

Mackenzie, Adrian, and Anna Munster. 2019. "Platform Seeing: Image Ensembles and Their Invisualities." *Theory, Culture & Society*. DOI: 10.1177/0263276419847508

Martin, Randy. 2002. *Financialization of Daily Life.* Philadelphia: Temple University Press.

Negri, Antonio. 2005. *The Politics of Subversion: A Manifesto for the Twenty-First Century.* Translated by James Newell. Cambridge: Polity Press.

Schapira, Michael, and Jesse Montgomery. 2017. "Stefano Harney (Part 1)." *Full Stop Quarterly,* August 8. http://www.full-stop.net/2017/08/08/interviews/michael -schapira-and-jesse-montgomery/stefano-harney-part-1/.

Srnicek, Nick. 2017. *Platform Capitalism.* Cambridge: Polity Press.

Authors

Timon Beyes is professor in Sociology of Organisation and Culture at Leuphana University Lüneburg and Copenhage Business School, and a director of Leuphana University's Centre for Digital Cultures (CDC). Recent related publications include the coedited *Oxford Handbook of Media, Technology, and Organization Studies* and "The Media Arcane," *Grey Room* 75 (with Claus Pias).

Lisa Conrad is academic councillor at the Institute for Sociology and Cultural Organization (ISCO) and postdoctoral research associate at the Centre for Digital Cultures (CDC) at Leuphana University Lüneburg.

Geert Lovink is a Dutch media theorist, internet critic, and author of *Uncanny Networks* (2002), *Dark Fiber* (2002), *My First Recession* (2003), *Zero Comments* (2007), *Networks without a Cause* (2012), *Social Media Abyss* (2016), and *Sad by Design* (2019). In 2004, he founded the Institute of Network Cultures at the Amsterdam University of Applied Sciences.

Reinhold Martin is professor of architecture at Columbia University. He cofounded the journal *Grey Room* and is author of *The Organizational Complex: Architecture, Media, and Corporate Space* (2003), *Utopia's Ghost: Architecture and Postmodernism, Again* (Minnesota, 2010) and *The Urban Apparatus: Mediapolitics and the City* (Minnesota, 2016).

Ned Rossiter is professor of communication at the Institute for Culture and Society, University of Western Sydney, and author of *Organized Networks: Media Theory, Creative Labour, New Institutions* (2006) and *Software, Infrastructure, Labor: A Media Theory of Logistical Nightmares (2016).*